Vegetable Soups from Deborah Madison's Kitchen

Vegetable Soups
from Deborah Madison's Kitchen

Deborah Madison

Broadway Books | *New York*

VEGETABLE SOUPS FROM DEBORAH MADISON'S KITCHEN. Copyright © 2006 by Deborah Madison. All rights reserved. No part of this book may be reproduced or transmitted in any form or by any means, electronic or mechanical, including photocopying, recording, or by any information storage and retrieval system, without written permission from the publisher. For information, address Broadway Books, a division of Random House, Inc.

PRINTED IN CHINA

BROADWAY BOOKS and its logo, a letter B bisected on the diagonal, are trademarks of Random House, Inc.

Visit our Web site at www.broadwaybooks.com

First edition published 2006

Book design by Elizabeth Rendfleisch
Photographs by Laurie Smith

Library of Congress Cataloging-in-Publication Data

Madison, Deborah.
    Vegetable soups from Deborah Madison's kitchen / Deborah Madison.—1st ed.
            p.   cm.
    Includes index.
    1. Soups.   2. Vegetable soup.   3. Vegetarian cookery.   I. Title.

TX757.M33   2005
641.8'13—dc22

                                        2005047050

ISBN 0-7679-1628-X

10   9   8   7   6

For my clay angels,
Judith
and
Vicki

contents

acknowledgments

Cooking is never a solitary endeavor, even when we're alone in our kitchens.

I'd like to acknowledge those who helped me create this collection of soups, starting with other cooks and writers whose ideas and approaches have, over many years, inspired my own recipes. There are a lot of you who have lived long on my library shelf, and I thank you all, but in particular writers Anne Bianchi, James Peterson, Kitty Morse, Lynn Rossetto Kaspar, Najmieh Batmanglij, Yamuna Devi, Rosita Arvigo, and Nadine Epstein for recipes that provided particular inspiration. I also want to thank Greg O'Byrne for his always good guidance in matters pertaining to wine.

I'm also grateful for the opportunity to have met a number of home cooks from farm-stays in Italy who have cooked their traditional soups and shared their techniques. They instilled in me the value and beauty of a well-crafted soup and the pleasure it brings to the human soul.

As always, I am indebted to my husband Patrick's seemingly endless patience with eating through the creative process book by book, especially soups, a food he has never been very fond of. I'm happy to report that he is much better disposed toward this "liquid food," so once again, Patrick, my deepest appreciation.

Food has to go into something, and I've been fortunate to have at my disposal, through the generosity of Judith Espinar, all the beautiful dishes and linens of The Clay Angel. Big bowls of thanks to Judith for her passion and her eye and of course to Linda Troynak, Lisa Kohl, and Denise Jones for graciously helping me once more to choose, wrap, and rewrap countless fragile items. In addition to the folk art ceramics from The Clay Angel, I was thrilled to add the extraordinary contemporary ceramics you see on these pages. Ceramist Vicki Snyder inspired this new direction, and I thank her for sharing her excitement along with her collection of modern ceramics and her own exquisite works.

Of course, these recipes would not have come so compellingly alive without Laurie Smith's beautiful photographs and the ever-expert help of Annie Slocum and Kathi Long, who made the intense days of shooting run smoothly and well.

I know that I'm speaking for all of us when I express my deep thanks to my neighbors, David and Vicki Snyder, for making their large summer garden available. Not only did we cook from their garden, but in between shots Laurie drifted out among the squash leaves, tomato vines, and flowers with her camera, photographing the raw material itself. My thanks to those two beautiful girls who were willing to sip soup for the camera, my neighbors Kylie and Frances O'Byrne.

Last, I wish to thank the all-important urban crew that dwells far from gardens and kilns but makes books such as this possible—my agent, Doe Coover; editor, Jennifer Josephy; publisher, Stephen Rubin; and all those who work hard to make ideas and manuscripts into those realities known as books.

*I*n many ways this has been the most enjoyable of all my books to write, be-cause so many people get nearly gushy about soup. When I said I was work-ing on a soup book, the response was often "Oh, I *love* soup!" People enthuse about soup in a way that's so heartwarming it makes me feel as if I'm in the right camp. After all, not everyone responded to my tofu book with cries of "I *love* tofu." Tofu is a food that many people have to learn to love. Soups are a shoo-in.

The cry of "I love soup!" comes from everywhere—meat eaters, vegetarians, col-lege kids and their parents, recent immigrants, blue bloods, artists, writers, bachelors. There's something about soup that makes it almost universally popular. Of course there are those who are far less enthusiastic about soup. I'm married to a man who sincerely asked at one point "Why would anyone want to eat wet food?" But even Patrick has come around to asking for a container of soup to take with him to his stu-dio, and he no longer flinches when I suggest a bowl of soup for dinner.

There are lots of reasons that soup finds such near-unanimous favor. For starters, there is something rather uncontrived about soup that's nice. There are a lot of dishes you can order from a contemporary American restaurant that lead you to expect one thing while being served something altogether different. The chef's style too often fails to match even our most basic expectations, which are apparently dull by comparison to his or her flights of fancy. But you can't mess up soup—not too much anyway. It's still going to be served in a bowl, and it will most likely be eaten with a spoon, and both of these attributes keep soup honest, regardless of other embellishments that may land on its surface. Soup is reliable, and in that alone we find a certain amount of comfort.

While it's possible to complicate anything in life, soup remains, for the most part, uncomplicated. Its ingredients are recognizable, and even its garnishes—croutons, swirls of pesto—are comfortably familiar. In a world of constant change, it's comforting to have a fallback kind of dish, and soup is it.

What else is there to like about soup?

It's a great stage for all kinds of vegetables, grains, and legumes to perform on. Perhaps there's no easier way to satisfy the now nine-a-day requirement than with a bowl of soup.

It's beautiful to look at, both in the making and in the bowl.

It's good any time of year, in any season, in any kind of weather, on any occasion. Soup is easy to make—doesn't take long or involve many steps—and with few exceptions soup gets better as it sits.

Leftovers are a boon, and variations made to a mother soup can keep you from getting bored with a large quantity. You can also freeze soups and pull them out to thaw as you need them.

Soup is inexpensive to make. And it's pretty low in calories as well—even if you finish it with a little cream, a swirl of crème fraîche, or a drizzle of fine olive oil. In the end, soup is still mostly water and fiber. And if you begin a meal with a soup, you'll start the main course already feeling satisfied, which can help you be moderate about what follows. At a special dinner, starting with soup slows everything down and makes the table that much more convivial.

For all of these reasons soup has become my lifesaver. I love to find it waiting for me in the fridge when I come in starving for lunch. I love knowing that I'm eating spinach and chard, beans, good grains, and other wholesome foods when I have a bowl of soup. I really like that even my richest soup isn't particularly caloric, that it takes just one bowl to make a meal, and that it takes only a few minutes to reheat. While it's an ideal food for those of us who work at home, it can also travel to work in a thermos, a great alternative to the snack machine or the eight-dollar sandwich. In short, every day is a good day for soup.

The soups in this book are based on vegetables, and many of these recipes are new ones for me. But some are soup classics, by which I mean both those that have stood the test of time in my kitchen (Quinoa, Corn, and Spinach Chowder) and those that are classics in the culture (Boston-Style Black Bean Soup). I've tried to streamline these dishes as much as possible without sacrificing goodness, so that you can easily enjoy them in your own kitchen. I hope you do enjoy making these soups and add them, one by one, to your repertoire.

I'VE ENJOYED making soups all my cooking life, time enough to come to a few conclusions about what ingredients contribute to a soup's goodness. Here's a look at some specifics.

Soup Basics: What Makes Vegetable Soups Good

Olive oil is the fat I use nearly all the time. I cook with a full-flavored olive oil that may or may not be labeled "extra virgin," but save my best extra virgin olive oil for drizzling over the surface of a finished soup. I've also found that dark sesame oil, usually used to finish a dish, can add heft to a soup and works well where its flavor is desired, such as the Adzuki Bean Soup with Celery Leaves and Sesame Rice Balls on page 52. Butter, allowed to brown before your soup vegetables are added, also brings a subtle, nutty layer of flavor to soups. The combination of dark sesame oil and brown butter has a mysterious flavor and a "meaty" quality that's not quite recognizable and is very good.

FAT

For years I've pretty much used 2 tablespoons of fat for 2 quarts of soup. That's less than a teaspoon per cup. Now I use more. Without the richness of chicken or meat stocks or even a good vegetable stock, which many cooks will be too busy to make, additional oil or butter and in some cases cream can be very effective in bolstering a soup's goodness. I don't make cream-based soups or soups thickened with egg yolks, but since I like to use enough fat for a soup to be satisfying, I've given a range of quantities in many recipes, such as 2 to 4 tablespoons olive oil. You can always use less if you wish. But if you use a very tiny amount of fat, know that you need to watch your pan like a hawk when browning vegetables as they will burn more easily.

Fat added at the end can often be a potent seasoning. I nearly always drizzle a teaspoon of olive oil into a bean soup at the table or shake a few drops of roasted sesame oil into a miso soup. When the oil meets the heat of the soup, its flavor simply blossoms. A tad of butter or a spoonful of cream added just before serving will do the same thing. You might want to think in terms of dividing the fat you use, using some to start the browning process and the rest to finish the dish.

As for milk, sour cream, yogurt, and other dairy, again the choice of low-fat, fat-free, or full-fat ingredients—or even nondairy versions of the same—is yours.

SALT

I tend to use 1 teaspoon sea salt for each quart of soup, which works out to ¼ teaspoon per cup. If you cook with chicken and meat stocks, you'll probably want to use less as they have their own natural salts, and bouillon cubes are notably salty. Sometimes I use more; other times less, depending on the soup itself. I usually start with a teaspoon early on in the cooking, then season to taste with more salt at the end. If I'm using a salted stock, I may not need to add more salt later. When it comes to bean soups, I usually let them cook for an hour before adding any salt as salt can slow down the softening process.

Like fat, salt is an ingredient for which we all have our own threshold of tolerance and desire. And of course what we're used to plays an important role. Food in Spain always seems very oversalted to me, but obviously not to those who live there. After a week at a spa, you may find that you've adjusted to the lower amounts of salt and fat used in spa cooking. If you are on a low-salt diet, the amounts I use will seem high. If you're used to salty stocks and other foods to begin with, they may seem low. In the end, it always has to be to your taste, which is why we always "season to taste" when finishing a dish.

SOUP STOCKS

Stocks are not difficult to make, and if you cook a lot, it becomes second nature to throw one together, even a quick little stock that underscores the principal ingredients in your soup. Still, it *is* an extra step, one I've tried to avoid to make these soups accessible to busy cooks. Many recipes don't need stocks, but there are those that are better with one and a few that actually require one.

If you like to use canned stocks and bouillon cubes, go ahead. Personally I'm not crazy about either. I don't find canned stocks as interesting as the quick ones you can make yourself, and bouillon cubes are always very salty and a little odd tasting. Prepared mushroom stock does have some virtue, though, and I turn to it in a pinch. As I do cook a chicken now and then, I make a stock from the leftovers, which can greatly enrich a soup, far more than the canned defatted, unsalted chicken stock, which tastes thin to me. If you're interested in learning how to build flavor through stocks, see pages 13 to 19.

BROTHS

A vegetable-based broth, a liquid you can enjoy even without a lot of other ingredients in it, is hard to come by. Broths take some concentration of materials, time, and thought. But because their lightness is welcome at times, it's been my challenge to develop a few recipes that will give you the vegetable equivalent of a consommé or brodo, a broth in which you can float a few noodles or vegetables. A good broth, of course, can always take the place of a less robust vegetable stock. The broths are found throughout the book:

Mexican Tomato Broth, page 29

White Bean Broth, page 36

Lentil Broth, page 38

Hearty Mushroom Broth, page 34

While a broth can stand on its own, there's no reason not to use any leftover broth as you would a stock. In fact, you can consider leftover broth a great bonus.

TEXTURE

Soups are either creamy, as in smooth, which doesn't necessarily mean cream is involved, or textured. A soup with chunks of things in it is usually more interesting to eat than a smooth one, but both have their place at the table.

A pureed, creamy-textured soup is often good served in small portions at the start of a meal. That way there's not so much that it becomes boring to eat. On the other hand, that smooth texture can be punctuated with things that make it interesting. Croutons, little cubes or thin slices of bread, crisped in olive oil or butter, are always good in a smooth soup. Or you can crown a smooth soup with little saladlike things—shaved vegetables, appropriate sprouts, such as sunflower seed sprouts in a Jerusalem artichoke bisque, or julienned apples and crumbles of cheese in a celery root soup. There are many quickly made things that you can use to add interest to a smooth soup or even build one into a meal.

The advantage of making a pureed soup is that it's easier than making one that won't be pureed: you can slice and chop your ingredients in rough chunks, since they're going to end up blended together. You can also rescue a soup that you cooked too long or one that just isn't very attractive, for whatever reason, by pureeing it. Here's the advice of a friend who is an excellent cook (and cookbook author): "When I'm not recipe testing, here's how I do soup: I take unidentified leftovers from the fridge, place them in a blender, add water, broth, or cream, and blend. Heat and you've got soup, but you never know what type. I've got a soup like this in my refrigerator, and when someone asked what it was at dinner last night, I said Brown Soup because I couldn't for the life of me remember what it was originally!" I've no doubt that coming from his kitchen, it was excellent. For the rest of us it might be better not to reveal your method if asked. People like to know what they're eating.

With soups that are meant to be textured, you have to take a little more care with both your cutting technique and your timing. You'll want your vegetables to look appealing; you'll want each to be cooked properly; and you'll want them to fit in your soupspoon, which means no overhanging slippery leaves that will be hard for the diner to manage. The advantages of such soups are that they are always interesting to look at and can present you with a world in a bowl through the layering of ingredients. You might puree a portion to give a little more cohesive background to all the parts, and if you've made a great deal of soup, you can always puree leftovers for variety.

A garnish is something you add for looks, like an unblemished sprig of cilantro, but finishing a soup is about adding those final elements that bring everything together and make it complete. Finishing can be as simple as swirling a spoonful of salsa verde or seasoned yogurt into a soup, or it can be a bit more complex, such as making mushroom duxelles and spreading them over toast or separately cooking barley, mushrooms, and leeks to give a creamy barley soup a bit of glamour. After making the stock and the body of the soup, finishing is the step that gives your soup the right dose of freshness, flavor, or texture, as well as style and panache.

FINISHING TOUCHES

Most of the recipes are for soups that can be simply ladled into a bowl, then finished. In such recipes, the serving amounts are given in cups or quarts. However, a few soups are composed of a number of elements (Summer Squash in Broth with Masa Dumplings and Cilantro Salsa, page 151), or even finished in the oven (Onion Panade with Olives and Lemon, page 101). For such soups, the number of servings the recipe makes is the amount indicated.

SERVING AMOUNTS

THIS INFORMATION will not be new to those who know my books. I've included it in one form or another in almost every one. The principles don't change much from year to year, yet there's some new material here, plus the basics for those of you who are first-time soup makers.

Making Vegetable Stocks: Some Guidelines

- Stocks are not a catchall for old or spoiled vegetables, but they can accommodate last week's carrots, mushrooms with open caps, *somewhat* wilted greens, and so on. If in doubt, ask yourself "Do I want to eat this?" If you don't, then don't put it in the stock.

- The more surface area exposed, the more quickly the vegetables yield their flavors, so roughly chop stock vegetables into pieces about an inch square.

- The more vegetable matter you use in proportion to water, the richer the flavor.

- Sautéing, roasting, and otherwise browning your vegetables first in a little oil adds more flavor to a stock. But you can skip this step if you want to and simply combine the vegetables and water before turning on the heat.

- Unlike meat stocks, vegetable stocks don't usually benefit from long hours of cooking. Quick stocks take 25 to 35 minutes, more basic stocks an hour or so, and broths, which are more intense, up to 2 hours, as in the Mexican Tomato Broth on page 29. You can concentrate stocks and broths further by simmering them, uncovered, once they are strained until the amount you need remains.

- Even after washing, some sand may remain embedded in the leaves and fissures of vegetables like leeks and celery root. Let the stock settle for a few minutes, then pour it carefully into a clean container. Don't let it sit for a long time, because certain herbs can turn bitter as they steep.

- Be cautious with unfamiliar herbs and vegetables. Some can turn grassy or bitter. If you're not sure about an ingredient, simmer it alone first, then take a sip to see if it's all right.

I think you'll find that making a stock is largely an intuitive process and often one that can take place right alongside preparing the vegetables for your soup. The guidelines and the list of stock elements on the following pages should help you approach stock making in a relaxed and spontaneous manner. In fact you may find, as I do, that it's a pleasure to use all the bits and pieces that might otherwise be thrown away and to end up with something that adds to the flavor of your final dish.

The generic vegetarian stock consisting of onion, carrot, celery, and bay leaf simmered in water doesn't add a great deal to a soup. There needs to be more, in the way of either ingredients or technique, to arrive at a liquid that adds something. But you can take even these most basic ingredients and tailor them to stocks that revolve around a constellation of particular ingredients and flavors by simply including pieces of the vegetables, herbs, and spices that work with your intended soup. If you're making a celery root and leek soup, for example, add the trimmings of these vegetables to the basic vegetables. Often simmering soup trimmings in water with onion, celery, carrots, and a handful of parsley can enhance your soup.

It's often more useful to know how ingredients work than to know a particular recipe, because then you can improvise with ease. Familiarize yourself with this material and you'll soon become adept at building flavor into your stocks and inventing new ones. The measurement suggestions, when given, are for 2 quarts of water.

Basic Ingredients for All Vegetable Stocks: Virtually all stocks start with these ingredients, which are the backbone ingredients for the basic Vegetable Stock on page 13.

Onions, leeks, carrots, celery
Thyme, bay, parsley, and garlic (use those little hard-to-peel cloves,
    which can be left unpeeled)
Leek and scallion trimmings: roots and leaves
Oil or butter for initial sautéing of the vegetables

Ingredients That Are Always Good to Include: These avoid the sweet end of the vegetable spectrum and give depth to stocks.

Chard stems and leaves, beet greens except for red ones
Fresh mushrooms, the soaking water from dried mushrooms,
    dried mushrooms
Scallions, in addition to or in place of onions or leeks
Potato parings and celery root skins *if* organic
Parsley root
Jerusalem artichokes
Lettuce
Eggplant

Lentils

Walnuts or almonds

Ingredients to Use for Their Particular Flavors: These ingredients have discernible flavors and should be included in stocks that will be used in soups that feature them.

Asparagus, the butt ends

Parsnips, trimmings and cores

Winter squash, skins and seeds

Fennel, stalks and trimmings

Corncobs and pea pods

Cilantro, lovage, Chinese celery

Cumin, ginger, lemongrass, galangal, saffron

Dried mushrooms

Ingredients for Summer Stocks: Vegetable stocks made in the summer can include any of the following seasonal vegetables and herbs *in addition to* the basic ingredients:

Zucchini and other summer squash

Tomatoes

Green beans and corncobs

Eggplant

Bell peppers: veins, cores, seeds, and discarded tops

Herbs: marjoram and basil, stems or leaves

Ingredients for Winter Stocks: Seek out these additions for your earthy winter vegetable stocks and add them to the basic ingredients.

Celery root parings, well scrubbed

Parsley root, burdock, and salsify

Leeks: paler green leaves and roots

Garlic, fresh or roasted

Dried or fresh sage, 1 or 2 teaspoons

Rosemary, about a 1-inch piece

Mushrooms, fresh and/or dried

Tomato paste

Lentils

Nonseasonal Ingredients That Add Depth to Stocks

Sprouted seeds and legumes, 1 to 2 handfuls

Lentils and mung beans, $\frac{1}{4}$ cup, rinsed

Cooking liquid from beans (in place of water), especially from chickpeas
   and white beans

Nettles, amaranth, and borage leaves, one or more handfuls

Miso, tamari, soy sauce: a spoonful at a time, to taste, at the end

Kombu, a 6-inch piece, added at the beginning

Nuts, $\frac{1}{2}$ to 1 cup, tied in cheesecloth, cooked for 20 minutes (they can be
   retrieved, dried in the oven, and used in cooking)

Rinds of Parmigiano-Reggiano

Ingredients to Avoid: There are very few ingredients to avoid, and almost all are vegetables in the cabbage family.

Turnips and rutabagas

Cabbages and Brussels sprouts

Broccoli and cauliflower, except stems

Red beets, unless you're making a beet soup

Tiny celery seeds, powdered herbs, ground pepper, because they can turn
   stock bitter

Artichoke trimmings, which are usually highly sprayed unless organic, and
   bitter

Funky, moldy vegetables (anything you wouldn't want to eat)

Vegetables that have been sprayed with pesticides and insecticides

Vegetable Stock

The steps in this basic stock can intermingle with the preparation of a soup as you'll be adding trimmings from the soup ingredients as you produce them. Begin making your stock before you organize your soup ingredients and it can be simmering while you prepare the soup vegetables.

As for the pot, what I'm calling a *stockpot* is simply a pot that is narrower than what you'd typically use for soup, which is a wide-bottomed pot more like a Dutch oven. However, since the volume is not likely to be more than 3 quarts, you needn't rush out and buy something special.

1 tablespoon olive or other oil suitable for the soup, optional
1 large onion, cut into ½-inch chunks
2 large carrots, chopped
2 celery ribs, including a few leaves, chopped
1 bunch of scallions, including half of the greens
6 garlic cloves, smashed
8 parsley sprigs with stems
6 thyme sprigs or ½ teaspoon dried
2 bay leaves
Additional soup vegetable trimmings, herbs, etc., if available
1 teaspoon sea salt

1. If you're using the oil, heat it in a stockpot, add the next 4 ingredients, and cook, stirring frequently, over medium-high heat for 10 minutes, or until they take on some color and glaze the pan. Then add the rest of the ingredients plus the water. If you're not using oil, put the ingredients in a stockpot and cover with 2 quarts cold water.

2. Take a look for other ingredients in your recipe that might amplify the soup—an herb that's called for, vegetable trimmings such as squash seeds and peels, or some-

thing from the garnish, such as scallion greens or chervil stems. Also check the refrigerator for useful tidbits—leftover chopped shallots, a lone mushroom, some chard stems, etc.—and add them to the pot.

3. Bring to a boil, then reduce the heat and simmer slowly, partially covered, while you go back to the soup. Give the stock at least 30 minutes if time allows, then strain it and add it to the soup. Still warm, it will quickly come to a boil.

Mushroom Stock

When there's a good price on mushrooms, I get half a pound or more and make this stock. It's not as substantial as the broth on page 34, but it provides a good fortification for many soups, such as the spinach soup on page 211.

To the following ingredients, add any of these vegetables should you have them on hand: parsnips, Jerusalem artichokes, leeks or leek roots and greens (about 1 cup), celery root or celery root trimmings.

1 to 2 tablespoons butter, olive oil, or a mixture
1 large onion, chopped
2 large carrots, sliced
2 celery ribs, including the leaves, chopped
2 large garlic cloves, smashed
2 thyme sprigs or $1/4$ teaspoon dried
2 bay leaves
Handful of coarsely chopped parsley
$1/2$ to 1 pound mushrooms, sliced
Sea salt and peppercorns
1 tablespoon tomato paste
$1/2$ cup red or white wine, optional
$1/4$ cup dried porcini
$1/4$ cup lentils or walnuts

1. Melt the butter or heat the butter and oil together in a stockpot. When hot, add the onion, carrots, celery, garlic, herbs, and any other vegetables you're adding. Cook over high heat, stirring occasionally, while you coarsely chop the mushrooms. Once they've taken on some color, after 5 minutes or so, add the mushrooms, salt, and peppercorns. Continue cooking over high heat for 3 or 4 minutes to sear the mushrooms, then stir in the tomato paste and work it into the vegetables. Add the wine, if using, and deglaze the pot, scraping up the juices from the bottom.

2. Add the dried mushrooms, lentils or walnuts, and 7 cups cold water. Bring to a boil, reduce the heat to a quiet simmer, and partially cover the pot. Cook for 45 minutes, then remove the lid and cook for 25 minutes longer to reduce. Strain the stock, pressing out as much liquid as possible.

Roasted Vegetable Stock

MAKES ABOUT
6 CUPS

Roasting intensifies the flavors of all vegetables and provides an easy way of bringing added character to what is essentially a basic vegetable stock. Especially nice to use in winter soups when you want a deeper layer of flavor.

4 large carrots
1 large celery rib with leaves
3 Jerusalem artichokes
1 large onion, cut into $1/2$-inch pieces
1 large leek, white part thinly sliced and rinsed, plus 1 cup chopped and rinsed
    inner greens
1 cup diced celery root
6 garlic cloves
2 tablespoons olive oil
2 teaspoons sea salt
$1/4$ teaspoon peppercorns

½ cup coarsely chopped parsley

2 bay leaves

Thyme sprig

4 sage leaves

1 teaspoon soy sauce, or as needed

1. Preheat the oven to 425°F and scrub the vegetables. Cut the carrots, celery, and Jerusalem artichokes into ¼-inch slices. Put them in a bowl with the onion, the white part of the leek, the celery root, and the garlic. Toss them with the oil, then spread on a sheet pan and roast, turning them every 10 minutes, until browned, about 40 minutes.

2. Transfer the roasted vegetables to a stockpot and add the remaining ingredients, except the soy sauce, plus 2 quarts cold water. Bring to a boil, then reduce the heat, partially cover the pot, and simmer for 40 minutes. Strain, pressing out as much liquid as possible. Taste for salt. A teaspoon of soy sauce may give the stock a little depth and additional saltiness.

Ten Steps to Making Vegetable Soups

CERTAIN STEPS are repeatedly encountered in soup making. I came up with these ten basic steps to explain how soups are made in *Vegetarian Cooking for Everyone.* Because they are basic, not much has changed since they were written, but they're still helpful for understanding the mechanics of soup making, especially for beginners. Once you're familiar with them and what they contribute, you can easily make soup without a recipe.

1. Warm the oil or butter. Fat captures the perfumes of herbs and garlic (the aromatics) and carries them throughout the body of the soup. They also contribute their own flavors to soups. Fat gets very hot, which is important for searing and browning onions and other vegetables, one of the first steps in making any soup. If you're on a diet, you might simmer the vegetables in stock or water, then add a small piece of butter or a few drops of oil to each bowl of soup—you'll get a lot of flavor for your calories this way.

2. Use a large, wide pot. A wide soup pot provides a generous surface area for the onions and vegetables to brown. If crowded on top of each other, they'll steam instead of brown. The soup pot should also have a heavy bottom so that the vegetables don't burn.

3. Add the onions or leeks. Alliums in some form—onions, leeks, shallots, or scallions—are almost always used to start a soup. They're cooked in oil or butter until they soften, often with aromatics such as parsley, bay leaf, thyme, garlic, and sometimes diced carrots and celery. It's important not to rush this step; the longer you give it, the better your soup will be. Browning onions contributes hearty flavor and rich color to the soup. When you want a more delicate flavor, cook your alliums more gently, over lower heat and for less time, and add a little water or stock after the first few minutes so that they stew rather than fry.

4. Cook until the onions are soft, 10 to 12 minutes. Onions take a while to break down, and their softening is inhibited by salt and acids, such as tomatoes, wine, vinegar, and lemon juice. It's good for the onions to be soft before salts and acids are added. If they're not, they can remain a bit raw tasting and in the worst case will float to the surface of the finished soup. Softening takes at least 10 minutes, but to be safe, plan on 12 or more, especially at higher altitudes.

5. Add the vegetables and salt. The remaining vegetables can be added to the onions or leeks once they have softened, along with some salt to bring out their flavors. Sometimes, however, they're added with the onions. It depends on the vegetable and the direction the soup is going in.

6. Add the water or stock. Now is the time to add the liquid to the vegetables. If you've made a quick stock, it will be warm. If you're using water, just add it cold from the tap. Scrape the pot to bring any of the glazed vegetable juices into the body of the soup.

7. **Boil, then simmer, partially covered.** The liquid needs to reach a boil, but constant boiling is too violent a motion for a good soup. Once the water or stock boils, lower the heat enough to produce a gentle and constant motion in the pot. The pot is usually covered, but not all the way, so that the soup doesn't escape in the form of steam, nor does it boil over. A little escaping steam keeps it all in check.

8. **Let cool, then blend or puree.** Many soups are pureed. They can be left with some texture or made silken by pureeing vigorously or straining the puree through a sieve. Mostly I use a blender because it's so reliable. But you can also use a handheld blender (a blender on a stick), a food processor, or a food mill. The latter is ideal for pureeing soups that are thickened with potatoes since potatoes can turn gummy when worked in a blender jar or food processor. The food mill is also the perfect tool for separating skins and fibers from the body of the soup. This way you could leave potatoes unpeeled and take advantage of their flavor, but when finishing the soup, leave the skins behind in the food mill.

   As boiling soups can sputter and burn, it's a good idea to let them cool a few minutes before pureeing in a food processor or blender. When using a blender, fill it no more than a third full and, as a safety precaution, lay a clean dish towel over the lid. Begin by blending with quick, little pulses or on the lowest speed until you've got the soup moving, then increase the ferocity of your blender. You can add more soup to the jar or work bowl while the machine is going.

9. **Taste for salt, season with pepper, and add a little lemon or vinegar.** If your stock was seasoned and you salted the vegetables, you probably won't need more salt at the end, but it's always a good idea to check right before serving. If the salt seems okay but the soup still needs *something,* often a little lemon juice or a splash of vinegar will bring all the flavors into sudden bright relief. Add chopped fresh herbs and freshly ground pepper just before serving even if you used them earlier. The heat of the soup makes both intensely aromatic.

10. Add the finishing touches and serve. **Soups often come in two parts: the body of the soup, then the little things that are added at the end to finish it—fresh herbs, cooked greens, croutons, cream, pepper, noodles, and so forth.** You can ladle out your soup and then add those touches that will contribute a harmonious or contrasting flavor, color, or texture. And if it's very cold or you live at high altitude where food cools quickly, take a moment to warm the empty soup bowls, either in a low oven or with hot water.

Wine and soup may not seem like a natural pairing for the simple reason that both are liquids. Certainly broths, thin soups, and consommés don't cry out for wine because their weights and textures are so similar to one another. But this isn't true with all soups.

Soups vary enormously in weight, complexity, texture, and ranges of flavors, and many soups are enjoyed as the heart of a meal. If you drink wine with your dinner, you'll probably want to be drinking wine with quite a few soups as well. At least I know that I do, and many of these soups are well suited to wine pairings. Wine authority Greg O'Byrne, my friend and neighbor, and I have come up with some suggestions that will help you enjoy your soups with a glass of wine.

*I*f you're a vegetarian who secretly envies those who can enjoy a *brodo* with pasta or sip on chicken soup when ill, you'll be happy to know that there are brothy vegetarian soups that can effect a cure or two. It's not easy to make a vegetable-based broth that's as robust as a good chicken broth, but it's possible to create a liquid that's good enough to be sipped and savored with a few additions for interest or amusement.

Developing vegetarian broths and broth-based soups has been a challenge, but I'm delighted with the results. They have depth of flavor, interest, and inherent lightness. Broth-based soups are appealing to those with small appetites, who are recovering from illness, or who are dieting, and they provide a light beginning to a large meal.

Restoratives are soups intended to help vanquish a cold or flu. In times when food wasn't as plentiful as it is today, restoratives were rich with cream, egg yolks, and meats, on the theory that calories and protein were needed to nurse a person to health. Twice I've had jobs that involved caring for women who were born before the turn of the century (the twentieth, not the twenty-first). When they were ill, they asked for chicken broth enriched with cream (plus curry powder) and eggs. One always asked for warm sherry beaten into egg yolks, with some cream thrown in at the end, a kind of zabaglione. I always made extra of that! Many soups, by virtue of being hot liquids, can work as restoratives, but the ones I've included here are especially known for their ability to make you feel better, no matter what ails you.

MAKES ABOUT
7 CUPS

Green Coriander and Ginger Broth
with tofu

Tofu soups don't always have to be miso based. Here tofu floats in a green broth infused with cilantro, scallions, and shiitake mushrooms. For extra flavor I add Chinese celery (see page 26), lovage, or the Japanese herb shiso to the soup as it simmers, then sprinkle a few drops of roasted peanut or sesame oil into each bowl once it's served.

Serve within an hour, and the green sparkle of the cilantro pervades. Although it's certainly best then, I don't hesitate to make a lunch of the leftovers for myself.

6 dried shiitake mushrooms

1½ tablespoons roasted peanut oil (page 24), plus extra roasted peanut or sesame
    oil to finish

2 slices fresh ginger, about 1½ inches wide, smashed

Sea salt

2 teaspoons finely diced jalapeño chile

2 teaspoons minced garlic

⅓ cup cilantro stems, finely chopped

2 bunches of scallions, including 2 to 3 inches of the greens, finely sliced

1 cup finely diced celery or thinly sliced Chinese celery

½ carton (8 to 10 ounces) soft tofu packed in water, drained and cut into small
    dice, or 1 aseptic box tofu, diced

½ cup chopped cilantro leaves

1 teaspoon soy sauce, or to taste, plus extra for serving

1. Cover the mushrooms with 5 cups boiling water and set aside while you dice and chop the vegetables.

2. Heat a soup pot over medium-high heat (I use a flat-bottomed wok-shaped pan here) and add the oil. When hot, add the ginger and $\frac{1}{2}$ teaspoon salt, give a stir, then add the chile and garlic and stir-fry for 2 minutes, adding the cilantro stems during the last 20 seconds or so. Reduce the heat to medium, add the scallions, and cook until bright green, about 3 minutes. Next add the celery, another $\frac{1}{4}$ teaspoon salt, then the soaking water from the mushrooms poured through a fine strainer, squeezing the mushrooms when you remove them from their water to get every little drop.

3. While the soup is simmering, thinly slice the mushroom caps and add them to the soup. Cook for 8 to 10 minutes. Add the tofu, give it 2 minutes to heat through, then add the chopped cilantro and soy sauce.

4. Serve the soup with a few drops of roasted peanut or sesame oil in each bowl and extra soy sauce for those who wish.

Roasted Peanut Oil

Loriva has made this oil for the past twenty years or so. I've been recommending it to readers since 1986. It has a big, full-blown scent of roasting peanuts that will truly astonish you. It takes any dish where it's used from blah to amazing. Loriva also makes fine roasted sesame oil and a passel of other oils, including walnut from California walnuts. Loriva oils can be found at supermarkets and specialty stores or online through www.loriva.com.

Chinese Celery and Shiitake Mushroom Broth
with thin somen noodles

Robust and lively Chinese celery is a boon in the kitchen. Not unlike lovage in flavor, it resembles celery, only the stalks are thin and wobbly rather than broad and crisp. You can find it at Asian markets and sometimes farmers' markets where there are Hmong and Vietnamese growers.

The broth simmers for thirty minutes, but after that the soup is done in the very few minutes it takes to cook the somen.

6 dried shiitake mushrooms
10 to 12 ounces (about 8 cups) Chinese celery, some of the more tender leaves set
    aside for garnish, the rest chopped
1 large bunch of cilantro, a small handful of leaves set aside for garnish, the rest
    chopped
2 bunches of scallions, chopped
2 slices fresh ginger, about 1½ inches wide, smashed
1 jalapeño chile, quartered and seeded
2 teaspoons chopped garlic
Sea salt
Juice and zest of 1 lemon, to taste
2 to 4 ounces thin somen noodles
Roasted sesame oil to taste

1. Cover the mushrooms with 1 cup boiling water and set them aside.

2. Put the Chinese celery, cilantro, scallions, ginger, chile, and garlic in a stockpot with ½ teaspoon salt. Add 2 quarts water, bring to a boil, then cover. Lower the heat and simmer for 30 to 40 minutes. Strain and return the stock to the stove. Pour the mushroom soaking liquid through a fine strainer into the stock. Thinly slice the mushrooms and add them to the broth as well. Add lemon juice to taste and season with salt.

3. Cook the somen in a quart of boiling water until tender, then drain and divide it among 4 bowls. Pour the broth over the noodles and add the lemon zest, juice to taste, and a few drops of sesame oil to each bowl, along with the reserved celery and cilantro leaves, minced.

Lovage and
Chinese Celery

Both plants have an untamed, assertive, and lively presence that I find exciting. You can count on them to wake up anything that is a little on the quiet side, such as bean- and grain-based dishes. Add a handful of leaves, chopped, to a pot of white bean soup and you have something that's familiar yet unusual.

In both lovage and Chinese celery it's the leaves that are used and primarily for flavor. The stalks of the latter are thin and fibrous, nothing you'd serve for an appetizer, but they certainly can be used to add robustness to a vegetable stock. It's the leaves that pack the final punch, though. They can be introduced to a soup during the cooking and at the end as a garnish.

For lovage you have to buy a start at a nursery, then take it home and plant it. Soon you'll have more leaves than you know what to do with. Chinese celery can be planted from seeds or, easier for most, bought at Asian markets that carry fresh produce.

MAKES ABOUT
6 CUPS

Golden Broth
with slivered peas, cucumber, and yellow pepper

The springboard for this soup is one of Yamuna Devi's recipes from her tome *Lord Krishna's Cuisine,* a book that offers many complex dishes to tempt the adventurous cook. Though this soup is surprisingly delectable even when made with water, the simple stock adds so much flavor that it's worth making. It requires forty minutes of unattended simmering for maximum flavor and can be made ahead of time, but the soup itself, which takes only fifteen minutes, should be made just before serving so that it will be vibrant and fresh. Serve over basmati rice if you wish and include a spoonful of yogurt. And do peel the pepper—it will taste so much better.

2 celery ribs, including some leaves, chopped

THE STOCK

1 large carrot, chopped

2 scallions

1 tablespoon coriander seeds

1 teaspoon cumin seeds

2 cloves

$\frac{1}{2}$ teaspoon peppercorns

1 cup diced fresh or canned tomatoes

1 teaspoon sea salt

Trimmings: a few sprigs of carrot tops; the top, ribs, and seeds of the bell pepper; a few pea pods; several tablespoons cilantro, dill, and parsley stems

1 large cucumber, peeled, halved lengthwise, and seeded

THE SOUP

Sea salt

2 tablespoons butter

1 carrot, cut into julienne strips

$\frac{1}{2}$ large yellow or orange bell pepper, peeled and finely slivered

$\frac{1}{2}$ teaspoon ground turmeric

$\frac{1}{2}$ teaspoon garam masala

$\frac{1}{4}$ teaspoon paprika

Handful of edible-pod or snow peas, finely slivered on the diagonal

1 heaping tablespoon *each* finely chopped mint, parsley, and cilantro

Juice of $\frac{1}{2}$ large lime (about 1 tablespoon), or to taste

$\frac{1}{2}$ teaspoon sugar

1 teaspoon finely diced jalapeño chile

$\frac{1}{2}$ cup cooked basmati rice, optional

TO FINISH

Yogurt or sour cream

Golden Broth with Slivered Peas,
Cucumber, and Yellow Pepper

1. Put the stock ingredients in a pot, add 6 cups water, and bring to a boil. Simmer, uncovered, for 40 minutes, then strain. You should have about 1 quart.

2. While the stock is simmering, cut the cucumber halves into thirds, put the pieces in a bowl with 1 teaspoon salt and water to cover for 20 minutes, then drain and slice thinly crosswise.

3. Melt the butter in a small soup pot. When hot, add the cucumber, carrot, bell pepper, turmeric, garam masala, paprika, and 1 teaspoon salt. Give a stir, cook for 2 or 3 minutes, then add the stock. Bring to a lively boil, then lower the heat and simmer for 8 minutes. Add the peas and cook for just 1 minute more, by which time the cucumbers should be tender and translucent.

4. Add the herbs, lime juice, sugar, and chile. Divide among 4 shallow bowls, add rice to each if you wish, and top with a dollop of yogurt or sour cream.

Mexican Tomato Broth

MAKES 2 QUARTS

Traveling in Mexico for the first time in the 1960s, I experienced many new flavors and dishes: a simple bowl of chicken broth with sliced onion, avocado, oregano, and lime floating in it; the famous *Caldo Tlalpeño* with its chickpeas, vegetables, and chile; and, of course, tortilla soups. This red vegetable broth supports soups like these with success, so it's well worth making if these are soups you enjoy.

The assembly is a snap—literally a matter of minutes. But it's a two-hour simmer that creates the depth you'll want. While the broth can be refrigerated, it loses its luster with each passing hour. So if you want to enjoy it adorned only with avocado and onion, plan to use it right away. For the tortilla soup on page 133 or the broth with dumplings and vegetables on page 151, it can be used later.

1 large onion, sliced

1 large zucchini, sliced

1 cup diced canned or fresh tomato

6 plump garlic cloves

1 large carrot or several smaller ones, sliced

3 celery ribs, chopped

1 or 2 big handfuls of cilantro

Large handful of parsley

Several chard or beet leaves

Handful of lentils

Several anise hyssop leaves or a good pinch of anise seeds

2 teaspoons dried Mexican oregano or 8 regular oregano sprigs

1 jalapeño chile, halved

2 teaspoons sea salt

1 teaspoon peppercorns, lightly crushed

Tomato paste to taste, optional

Put all the ingredients except the tomato paste in a pot with 3 quarts water. Bring to a boil, then lower the heat. Simmer, partially covered, for 2 hours, then strain. Taste for salt and, if you wish to fortify the flavor a bit, stir in a teaspoon or more tomato paste to taste.

MAKES 4 TO 6 CUPS

Mexican Tomato Broth
with avocado and lime

This light soup might open a dinner or suffice for someone with a small appetite. Add heat to your liking with some finely sliced serrano chiles or a dab of pureed chipotle chile in adobo sauce.

4 to 6 cups Mexican Tomato Broth (page 29)

1 large avocado, peeled and sliced

1/4 cup finely sliced white onion

Several pinches of dried Mexican oregano
1 serrano chile, thinly sliced, or a scant teaspoon pureed canned chipotle chile in
    adobo, to taste, optional
1 lime, quartered

Heat the broth. Divide it among 4 bowls and divide the avocado among them.
Add some onion and a pinch of oregano to each bowl. Add the chile if desired
and serve with the lime on the side.

Cauliflower
in a saffron broth

Herb and Garlic Broth and White Bean Broth both make good bases for this light
and appealing soup. The pale green cauliflower (broccoflower) and the lime-green
whorls of broccoli Romanesco are both stunning in this golden broth, but plain
white cauliflower is just fine too. A mixture, of course, is particularly lovely.

5 to 6 cups Herb and Garlic Broth (page 43) or White Bean Broth (page 36)
Pinch of saffron threads
2 teaspoons extra virgin olive oil
2 cups very small broccoflower or broccoli Romanesco florets
1/2 cup linguine or pastini, cooked separately in boiling salted water
Small pinch of hot red pepper flakes
Sea salt and freshly ground pepper
1 teaspoon minced parsley
Parmigiano-Reggiano for grating

Heat the broth with the saffron and olive oil in a soup pot. Add the broccoflower
and simmer until tender, after 8 or 10 minutes. Add the cooked pasta, pepper
flakes, and parsley. Taste for salt, season with pepper, then serve with plenty of
cheese grated into each bowl.

Garden Soup with Black Kale and Cauliflower
from the Veneto

MAKES ABOUT
2 QUARTS

The garden in this case was in northern Italy, at a farmhouse where four of us spent several days one November. In our party was a vegan who insisted on eating Italian food without meat, cheese, or eggs. As a result, we often ended up eating what he ate, and in this particular *agriturismo* our hostess made this very good soup with vegetables from her garden. However, it was even better with the addition of the local Asiago cheese, which, fortunately, she placed on the table.

2 fat leeks, white parts only, diced (about 2 cups)

I russet potato (about ½ pound)

2 tablespoons olive oil, plus extra to finish

2 cups stemmed and slivered cavolo nero (black kale)

About 2 cups small cauliflower florets

I garlic clove, minced or pressed

Sea salt and freshly ground pepper

6 cups White Bean Broth (page 36) or Vegetable Stock (page 13), made with the
   trimmings

Asiago cheese for grating

You can make this soup with water, the bean broth, or, if you're not a vegetarian, chicken stock. Or make a stock with the trimmings of the leeks and potatoes, and you'll end up with a surprisingly full-bodied soup that doesn't require a day or two of maturing.

1. Wash the diced leeks well. Chop the potato, leaving the skin on if you like if it's organic. Warm the olive oil in soup pot over medium heat. Add the leeks and the potato, give them a stir, and while they're warming up, slice the kale off its ropy stems, then slice the leaves into short ribbons. Add the kale to the pot along with the cauliflower, garlic, and salt. Cook for about 5 minutes.

2. Add the stock, bring to a boil, then lower the heat and simmer until the vegetables are tender, about 20 minutes.

3. Ladle the soup into bowls and drizzle some olive oil into each. Season with pepper and grate a little cheese into the soup, unless, of course, you don't eat dairy.

light broths and restorative soups

Hearty Mushroom Broth

MAKES 1 QUART

This is not an instant preparation. It takes time to tease out all the possibilities the ingredients offer, but that's what makes this rich broth so special. The flour gives it just a bit of body. I use porcini when I want an Italian flavor and shiitake if I plan to go more in an Asian direction.

You can do a lot with this robust broth, convincingly meaty in character. It can become the liquid for a vegetable pot-au-feu, page 179. It can support some tender dumplings. Or you can serve it as is with toasted croutons. It keeps well for a week in the refrigerator, and it can be frozen, something I make a point of doing since even a cup is excellent for boosting a simple mushroom soup to excellence.

½ to 1 cup dried porcini or shiitake mushrooms
1 tablespoon butter
4 teaspoons light sesame or olive oil
1 large onion, chopped
1 large carrot, chopped
2 celery ribs, diced
1 small parsnip, peeled and chopped
½ pound fresh mushrooms and/or mushroom trimmings such as stems, broken
    caps, etc.
4 garlic cloves, smashed
Aromatics: 4 thyme sprigs, 1 bay leaf, a 2-inch rosemary sprig
Sea salt and freshly ground pepper
1 heaping tablespoon tomato paste
1 tablespoon flour
2 cups dry red wine
1 heaping tablespoon dark miso, or more to taste

1. Cover the dried mushrooms with 6 cups warm water and set aside. Melt the butter in a wide soup pot until it browns and smells nutty, then add the oil, vegetables, garlic, and aromatics. Cook over medium-high heat, stirring occasionally, until the vegetables are well browned, 15 to 20 minutes. Season with 1 teaspoon salt and a little pepper.

2. Stir in the tomato paste and flour, then pour in the wine. Raise the heat and boil for about 2 minutes, vigorously scraping the bottom of the pot to work in the juices, then add the dried mushrooms and their soaking liquid. Bring to a boil, lower the heat, and simmer, covered, for 45 minutes. Strain into a 1-quart mea-

sure. You should have 1 quart. At this point you can use the broth, refrigerate it for up to a week, or freeze it.

3. Just before using, mix the miso with a little hot broth, return it to the pan, then heat it nearly to boiling.

I'VE LONG BEEN a fan of bean broths, which is one of the reasons I originally bought a pressure cooker. I figured that I could quickly cook my own beans and have the use of their savory broth in no time at all. But bean broths certainly didn't originate with me. They have a name, *acqua pazza,* "crazy water," according to Lynn Rossetto Kaspar—crazy because you can make something delicious out of nothing but water, beans, and a few aromatics.

One of the nice things about having a bean broth on hand is that it can easily be turned into a light meal for one or two people. You can cook it, a portion at a time, adding small treasures—say a sliced cooked artichoke heart or some ravioli, a few leaves of spinach or chard, some noodles or dumplings, a fluffy mound of Parmesan, or strips of kale and a dice of root vegetables. And, of course, you can use it as a fortifying stock for a vegetable soup.

While white beans yield a versatile golden broth, you need not be limited to white bean broths. One made from black beans is delicious seasoned with cumin, cilantro, and a little chipotle puree, with rice added for texture. Lentil broths are good with herbs like sorrel or chives, spinach, a spot of cream, and some crunchy croutons. And all bean broths can be thickened by pureeing some of the beans and adding them back to the pot. Even so, you'll have cooked beans left over. You can use them in various ways: add them to the broth for texture, use them in a salad if they're not too soft, make a warm puree with olive oil and rosemary to spread on toast, or serve them as a side dish with butter or olive oil, salt and pepper, and a bit of herb, such as parsley or summer savory.

White Bean Broth

The parsnip gives this broth a "meaty" flavor, well suited for the chilly months of the year.

1 cup dried white beans
3 tablespoons butter or olive oil
1 onion, chopped
1 large carrot, sliced
1 large celery rib, chopped
2 leeks, the roots scrubbed and white parts chopped
1 parsnip, peeled and diced
3 large garlic cloves, smashed
1 thyme sprig or a couple pinches of dried
1 branch sage leaves (about 8 leaves)
Sea salt
6 large parsley branches
2 cloves
Tomato paste to taste

1. Cover the beans with boiling water and set them aside while you wash and chop the vegetables.

2. Melt the butter or heat the oil in a soup pot or pressure cooker over low heat. Add the onion, carrot, celery, leek roots and white parts, parsnip, garlic, thyme, and sage. Cook gently and slowly, stirring occasionally, until the onion is pale gold and smells good, about 20 minutes. Add a teaspoon of salt.

3. Drain the beans and add them to the pot along with the parsley, cloves, and 10 cups water. Bring to a boil, then simmer, covered, either in a regular pot for 2 to 3 hours or in a pressure cooker on high pressure for 40 minutes. When done, strain. You should have about 7 cups or more. Boil to reduce the amount to a quart. Taste for salt. Work in tomato paste to taste for both color and flavor.

Add cooked ravioli, fine noodles, or small dried pasta shapes and finish with a sprinkling of parsley and a little freshly grated Parmesan.

White Bean Broth with Pasta

Simmer strips of chard, kale, or other greens in the broth with a chunk of Parmesan cheese rind, a few tablespoons of the cooked beans, and a fine dice of carrot, turnip, or celery root, until the greens are tender. Finish with grated cheese and a few drops of olive oil.

White Bean Broth with Greens, Beans, and Parmesan Cheese Rind

To each bowl, add chunks of boiled or steamed potatoes, a thread of olive oil, or a bit of good butter, a pinch of parsley, and a shower of freshly grated Parmigiano-Reggiano. Use some of the beautiful heirloom potatoes—pink, violet, or blue— as well as yellow-fleshed fingerlings.

White Bean Broth with Boiled Potatoes

Add a pinch of nutmeg to the broth and serve with good bread, toasted, brushed with olive oil, and lightly rubbed with garlic floating in the soup, again with good Parmesan cheese grated over all.

White Bean Broth with Bread

Using real Parmigiano-Reggiano is a necessary luxury in my kitchen—it's just that good. Usually I use it freshly grated over something hot—a soup, pasta, or other dish—an opportunity for its nutty aroma to fully bloom. The rinds go into soups, where they add a great deal of flavor, so there's no waste. There are other cheeses made in the Parmesan style, of course, that are less expensive, and they can also be used. Or you may go back and forth between a lesser-quality Parmesan and the real thing, saving the good stuff for those dishes where you feel it really counts. In either case, what matters most is to grate your own cheese as you need it and forgo buying dried-out, pregrated cheese, even if it is Parmigiano-Reggiano.

Parmigiano-Reggiano

Lentil Broth
with scallions and crème fraîche

Before it's finished, you might think that this dark broth is a bit pedestrian. But stir in the cream, add slivered scallions and the butter-crisped croutons, and suddenly you have a broth that you can't quit sipping.

The lentils themselves can be turned into a side dish or a salad, so choose them according to what you want to do with them later. I often cook a mixture of black and green lentils, which hold their shape well. If you're not ready to use the cooked lentils, simply freeze them until you are.

1 tablespoon olive oil
1 small red onion, finely diced
$\frac{1}{3}$ cup *each* finely diced celery and carrot
2 bay leaves
$\frac{1}{2}$ cup chopped parsley
2 tablespoons tomato paste
2 garlic cloves, minced
1 cup lentils, sorted and rinsed
Sea salt and freshly ground pepper
2 slices country bread, cut into tiny cubes
1 tablespoon butter
$\frac{1}{4}$ cup crème fraîche or cream
4 scallions, including an inch of the greens, thinly sliced

1. Heat the oil in a soup pot over medium-high heat. Add the onion, celery, carrot, bay leaves, and parsley. Sauté until the onion begins to color around the edges, about 7 minutes, then work the tomato paste into the vegetables, add the garlic, and cook for 2 minutes longer. Add the lentils, 5 cups water, and 1 teaspoon salt. Bring to a boil, then lower the heat and simmer, partially covered, until the lentils are tender, about 35 minutes.

2. Pour the lentils into a colander set over another pot and return the broth to the stove. Crisp the bread cubes in the butter over medium-low heat until golden,

about 6 minutes. Whisk the crème fraîche with some of the broth and stir it into the soup along with the scallions. Taste for salt. Ladle the soup into mugs or bowls, add the croutons, season with pepper, and serve.

CERTAIN SOUPS have always made their mark as restoratives and curatives, soups that nurture us back to health or turn away an impending cold or flu. Chicken stock is best known for this, but these broths can be of help, too. It turns out that they are all soups full of flavor, satisfying enough to work well as dieters' soups for those times when you want to shed a few pounds.

Restoratives

Delicious Dieter's (or Sick Person's) Soup

MAKES ABOUT
10 CUPS

When I said I felt fluish one winter night, my friend, a cinematographer who had just finished shooting a movie in snow, rain, and freezing rushing water, said, "What you need is Sick Person's Soup." A fax arrived the next morning, and I set to work. While making it I thought, You'd have to be sick to eat this—no salt, no butter, no oil—or on a very determined diet. But it fools you. By the time you stir in the garlic, ginger, lime, and white miso, you have quite a robust soup. And besides, when you're sick, you don't want salt and fat and all of that, nor do you want it when you're dieting. What you want are flavor and vigor, and this soup has plenty of both. But I do add a few drops of roasted sesame oil to each bowl for an extra boost of flavor.

4 cups (about 10 ounces) chopped green cabbage

2 small celery ribs, diagonally sliced

1 small onion, thinly sliced

1 medium carrot, thinly sliced

12 garlic cloves, 6 sliced and 6 finely chopped

The original recipe, from *Rainforest Home Remedies* by Rosita Arvigo and Nadine Epstein, made a huge amount. I've made a more manageable amount here so that the miso, one of the agents of health, doesn't have to be reboiled indefinitely. The essential idea remains true to the original.

4 tablespoons grated ginger
1 chile, seeded (or not) and diced
Juice of 1 lime
⅓ cup white miso
Few drops of roasted sesame oil

1. Bring 6 cups water to a boil in a soup pot. Add the cabbage, celery, onion, carrot, and sliced garlic. Cover and cook for 20 minutes.

2. Stir in the chopped garlic, ginger, and chile and turn off the heat. Squeeze in the lime juice. Add the miso directly to the pot or dissolve it first in a cup with a little of the liquid, then pour it into the soup. Taste and add more if needed. Serve yourself a big bowl and feel better. If you're feeling fine and want a bit more flavor, shake a few drops of sesame oil into your soup.

MAKES 7 CUPS ## Broccoli Soup
with garlic, ginger, and chile

Here's another soup that will pick you up when you're down with a cold, but it's also a great little soup for when you're feeling fine. It's a lovely shade of green, on the thin side rather than dense, and utterly invigorating. I drink it right out of a cup, seasoned only with a few drops of roasted peanut oil (page 24), although you can swirl in some cilantro salsa if you want something fancier. If you cut everything very finely and with care, you can leave the soup unpureed, keeping the florets of broccoli and green disks of the stems in view.

Broccoli is of course one of those super vegetables that we should eat every day, but also one of the most heavily sprayed, so make sure you go for organic.

Scant 2 pounds broccoli (3 or 4 broccoli "trees")
1 tablespoon light sesame or sunflower seed oil

1 onion, thinly sliced or finely diced

1 large garlic clove, chopped

1 jalapeño chile seeded and diced

A 1-inch knob of ginger, peeled and chopped (about 1 tablespoon)

$^{1}/_{4}$ cup minced cilantro stems or chopped cilantro leaves

1 small potato, grated

Sea salt

2 tablespoons white miso

Roasted sesame or peanut oil (page 24) for serving

1. Separate the broccoli crowns from the stalks and cut them into florets more or less the same size, small or large. Thickly peel the stalks so that none of the thick fibrous outer layer remains, then slice them thinly.

2. Heat the oil in a wide soup pot. When hot, add the onion, garlic, chile, ginger, and cilantro and sauté, stirring rapidly, for 1 minute. Add the potato and broccoli stems, season with a scant teaspoon salt, add 2 cups water, and simmer, covered, until the onion is soft, about 5 minutes. Add the broccoli florets and 4 cups water and simmer just until the broccoli is tender, 5 to 10 minutes once it comes to a boil. Let cool briefly, then puree until smooth, leaving only minuscule nubbins of broccoli.

3. Mix the miso with some of the soup to dilute it, then pour it back into the pot. Taste for salt. Serve with a few drops of sesame oil in each bowl.

Herb and Garlic Broth
(aigo bouido)

The health-giving quantities of sage and garlic make this Provençal Herb and Garlic Broth a great comfort to one with a cold or flu. And for those in the best of health, it simply tastes good.

For me, Aigo Bouido has stood the test of time. At Greens I served it with garlic-rubbed croutons, chunks of new potatoes, or tender ravioli to start an evening meal. It has also doubled as a soup stock on countless occasions, and today it still serves me well. After all, it's hard to arrive at a golden vegetable broth with robust flavor in less than 30 minutes, and this does exactly that.

Big head of garlic, preferably a fresh, firm hard-necked variety
6 sage leaves
2 bay leaves
2 thyme sprigs
2 parsley branches
Sea salt and freshly ground pepper
Your favorite full-flavored olive oil to taste

Put 5 cups water in a soup pot over a high heat. Separate the garlic cloves, peel them, and add them along with the herbs and ½ teaspoon salt. Bring to a boil and cook, covered, for 20 minutes, then strain into a clean pot or simply remove the herbs, leaving the pearly garlic cloves if you wish. Taste for salt, season with pepper, and add 1 or 2 teaspoons olive oil to the pot. You can now enjoy this as a broth, use it as the base for a soup, or enhance it with various additions.

Use a good, firm head of garlic with no bruised, softened, or sprouting cloves. When the soup is done, you can float them right in the broth or you can press them through a strainer, which makes your broth a little cloudy but very tasty.

Cook 2 ounces noodles separately in salted water, then drain and add to the broth. Add a pinch of chopped parsley and grate over a little Parmesan cheese. The pasta might be a swirl of thin vermicelli, skinny broken egg noodles, or a fanciful pasta such as saffron linguine.

Herb and Garlic Broth with Pasta

Toast 3 or 4 slices of firm white bread or rustic country bread. Rub with garlic, then cut into little pieces. Divide among 4 bowls, cover with the broth, add fresh pepper and parsley, and serve.

Other Serving Ideas

- Add chunks of steamed or boiled potatoes to each bowl.
- Serve with several small ravioli or a single big luscious one filled with mashed potato or ricotta cheese.
- Wilt ribbons of spinach or chard leaves in the broth and add potatoes or croutons.

MAKES ABOUT
10 CUPS

A Spring Tonic

Too many meals eaten out or general overindulgence can create an appetite for this nourishing soup of herbs and greens. It soothes an unhappy tummy and makes you feel, well, just better. It's quite delicious when you're in the pink, too.

This soup uses herbs (sorrel, arugula, borage), wild greens (nettles), and oddities (radish and carrot tops)—and more familiar beet greens, all virtuous and good to eat. It can absorb numerous greens or succeed with a smaller selection, but whether there's a predominance of bitterness (from escarole), sharpness (from sorrel), or indeterminate wildness—from nettles, quelites (wild spinach), and the like—will depend on your own leanings. When they all come together in a single pot, the sum of the flavor is always larger than the parts.

2 tablespoons olive oil or butter, plus extra for serving
2 small potatoes, diced
1 large onion, diced
2 carrots, diced
5 garlic cloves, chopped
A bushy thyme sprig or a few pinches dried
Handful of parsley
Handful of watercress

2 cups blanched chopped nettles, if available, or extra watercress
2 cups sorrel, chopped
2 cups chard, beet greens, wild spinach (quelites), or amaranth
1 or 2 handfuls of odd greens: several borage leaves, radish tops, carrot tops
Sea salt and freshly ground pepper
Fresh lemon juice or vinegar to taste

Extra virgin olive oil or crème fraîche TO FINISH
Chive blossoms or wild mustard petals, if available

1. Warm the oil in a wide soup pot. Add the potatoes, onion, carrots, garlic, thyme, and parsley. Give a stir, cook over medium heat for several minutes, and then add the greens. Season with $1\frac{1}{2}$ teaspoons of salt. Cook over medium heat until the greens have collapsed, about 5 minutes, turning them every so often.

2. Once the greens have wilted, add 2 quarts water. Bring to a boil, then lower the heat and simmer until the potatoes are soft, 25 minutes or so. Cool briefly, then puree, either leaving the soup with some texture or making it smooth.

3. Taste for salt, season with pepper, and add a little lemon juice or vinegar to sharpen the flavors. Finish with a swirl of extra virgin olive oil or a little crème fraîche and, if possible, chive blossoms or the yellow petals of wild mustard.

White Miso Soup
with red dulse and ginger

MAKES ABOUT
1 QUART

White miso is the most sweet and delicate of the various miso pastes, and I've recently taken to it with a passion. It makes a lovely soup on its own and does wonders for other soups, seasoning them without overwhelming them.

While you can stir miso into water and have an invigorating broth in mo-

ments, it's even better if you take a few minutes to make a dashi, or stock, of kombu, a sea vegetable, and shaved flakes of bonito, both of which can be bought at health food stores and Asian markets. Since many so-called vegetarians do eat fish, I include this simple recipe for dashi. Dulse, a delicate red sea vegetable, floats in the soup—a lovely contrast of color and taste—and ginger lends its heat, making this a restorative soup even if you don't need any shoring up. There's no reason not to include tiny cubes of soft tofu as well.

Both dashi and miso soups are very simple to make, so don't try to make them ahead of time. They're clearly best made *à la minute*.

2 strips kombu, each about 6 inches long	THE DASHI
1 cup bonito flakes, loosely measured	

4 thin slices fresh ginger	THE SOUP
½ cup white miso	
1 cup firm or soft tofu, cut into tiny cubes	
Handful of red dulse (about 12 pieces), covered with warm water	
Few drops of roasted sesame oil to taste	
2 scallions, sliced diagonally into thin strips	

1. To make the dashi, put the kombu in a saucepan with 1 quart water and gradually bring it to a boil. Simmer for 1 minute, then remove the kombu. Add the bonito flakes, turn off the heat, let stand for 4 minutes, then strain.

2. Return the dashi to the pot and add the ginger. Warm over low heat. Mash the miso paste with enough of the dashi to make a thick cream. Return this to the soup, add the tofu, and continue heating. When the tofu is hot throughout, it will rise to the surface, but try not to let the miso boil. Boiling degrades its quality. Taste and make sure that it's strong enough for you. If not, add more miso. Strain the dulse and add it to the soup.

3. Ladle the soup into bowls or cups, dividing the tofu and dulse among them. Add a few drops of sesame oil to each bowl, garnish with the scallions, and serve.

What's not to like about a robust soup made of beans unless, of course, you're one who doesn't like beans to start with? Such people do exist (I'm married to one), and this chapter won't be their favorite. But those of us who find bean-based soups hearty, filling, and good tasting will be pleased. On the good-for-you side of the equation, bean soups, or beans alone, are high in protein and long on fiber. Of course there's bound to be a drawback to something with so many virtues: beans take forethought and time. Fortunately, bean soups get better as they age. Since they *are* a bit of hassle, these recipes, with few exceptions, make a lot—$2^{1}/_{2}$ to 3 quarts. The soups can be eaten over the week; they can be frozen; and they can be finished in different ways, so that they don't get boring as you make your way through them.

Bean soups don't require a stock; in fact they make their own as they cook, especially if you add some herbs, garlic, and olive oil. And you can even cook beans without having a plan in mind. You'll have plenty of time to decide what you want to do with them once they're done, even if it's just freezing them for another occasion. And if you want to use canned beans, read on.

Bean Basics BEANS ARE BETTER if they've been soaked, and once they have been, they take about 1½ hours to cook. *Exactly* how long depends on the kind of beans, how old they are, and the hardness of your water and your altitude, which affects the temperature at which water boils. This time can be shortened if you use a pressure cooker. In fact, beans can go from hard pebbles to soft legumes in the space of an hour in a pressure cooker, and today's versions are a snap to use. They won't blow up on you like our grandmother's did.

If you work at home, you can easily fit bean soups into your schedule, especially if you tend to wander into the kitchen for a look in the fridge every hour or so. In that case, bean soups are made for you. Put some beans on to soak, come back in an hour, put them on to cook, and before you know it, they'll be done and you've got dinner made.

Soaking AS FOR SOAKING BEANS, there are two methods: the quick soak and the overnight soak. When recipes call for soaked beans, either method can be used. Whichever you choose, look through your beans for any bits of chaff or small stones. Remove such detritus and rinse the beans well.

For a *quick soak,* bring water to a boil, about a quart per cup of beans. Add the beans, boil for one minute, turn off the heat, and cover the pot. In an hour they will have plumped up to thrice their volume.

For an *overnight soak,* first know that it needn't be really overnight as long as it's at least four hours. Cover your sorted beans with plenty of water and set them aside for at least that long.

It's also possible to skip soaking altogether. But the beans will take longer to cook and will absorb three times their volume in liquid, which you need to take into account.

Dried Beans or Canned? IN GENERAL, I prefer using dried beans over canned because I want the broth that they yield, because my beans won't be overcooked, and because I can use the types of beans I want to use, such as unusual heirloom beans or varieties that aren't available canned. Also, there is something very satisfying about providing the gentle long simmer that nudges beans to perfection. Though far from a gentle nudging, beans cooked under pressure can also yield a wonderful-tasting soup, and many people appreciate a fully cooked, soft bean. With a pressure cooker, you can still use the beans you want to cook *and* end up with a tasty broth.

While I'm not wild about canned beans, they are not a complete anathema either. They're far better than they used to be, and today more varieties of beans are available than in the past. Plus many brands are now organic and free of the ingredients that give canned beans an off taste. In spite of these improvements, canned beans are generally overcooked. Still, there are some soups in which canned beans fare well. One category is soups that include a lot of other elements so that the overall quality of the soup isn't compromised. Another is pureed bean soups that use a stock or broth.

Canned chickpeas, I might mention, are generally not as overcooked as other legumes. This is good, because chickpeas can take a notoriously long time to cook. For this reason, I often use canned ones in soups—I can relax about the timing and simply add them at the end. (If you have a fiddly nature, pinch the skins off the chickpeas before adding them to the soup—a step that improves both flavor and appearance.) However, there are times when I do make a chickpea soup from scratch, as in the Chickpea and Spinach Soup with Bread Crumbs on page 68, because the flavor is truly astounding, nothing like what comes out of a can. It's important to be reminded now and then what the difference really is: it's big, and I would hope that we don't forget—or worse, never learn—what cooked-from-scratch tastes like.

If you want to make a soup using canned beans, here are some useful things to know.

1. One cup dried beans swells to $2\frac{1}{2}$ cups cooked, while one 15-ounce can of beans equals about $1\frac{1}{2}$ cups cooked, so for every cup of dried beans called for, just plan to use 2 cans. It's a little more than the exact equivalent, but not enough extra to be worth saving.

2. Because most canned beans are overcooked, use them in soups where they're going to be pureed or added at the last minute.

3. If using canned beans, you might want to use a stock. For every can of beans, you'll need about 3 cups of stock to bring them to a souplike consistency.

Adzuki Bean Soup
with celery leaves and sesame rice balls

Adzuki beans are small and red and, like other red beans, on the sweet side. That's why sharp fresh celery leaves are so good here. In fact, adzuki beans are used—with added sugar—to make a sweet soup in China and delicious pastries in Japan. They're delicate and a little different from other beans. Once you've encountered them, you'll always be able to recognize their unique flavor.

Leave the soup with the beans in it or puree some or all of them. Either way, this is a good soup to serve with a ball of sesame-coated rice, in this case sweet white or brown rice (page 53).

THE BEANS

1 cup adzuki beans, soaked
1 tablespoon roasted sesame oil, plus extra to finish
1 small onion, finely diced
1 carrot, finely diced
2 celery ribs, finely diced
1 bay leaf
2 tablespoons mirin
Handful of celery leaves, chopped with a few parsley leaves
Sea salt and freshly ground pepper
1 tablespoon white miso, or to taste

THE RICE

1 cup short-grain sweet brown or white rice
$^{1}/_{2}$ cup sesame seeds, toasted in a dry skillet until golden

1. Drain and rinse the beans, then set them aside.

2. Heat the oil in a soup pot over medium heat. Add the onion, carrot, celery ribs, and bay and cook gently, stirring occasionally, for about 15 minutes. Add the mirin and allow to cook away, then add the beans, half of the chopped celery leaves, and 6 cups water. Bring to a boil, lower the heat, and simmer, covered, for an hour. Add 1$^{1}/_{2}$ teaspoons salt and continue cooking until the beans are soft, an-

other 15 to 30 minutes. Remove the bay leaf and puree a cup or all of the beans. Stir in the miso, taste for salt, and season with a little pepper.

3. Cook the rice in 2 cups simmering salted water until tender. Let it cool a little, then rinse your hands in cold water and, without drying them, form a small handful of rice into a ball, making one for each person. Roll the balls in sesame seeds to coat. Or toss the rice with the sesame seeds, then use an ice-cream scoop to form a ball. Ladle the soup into shallow soup bowls, sprinkle with the remaining chopped celery leaves, add a rice ball and a few drops of roasted sesame oil to each, and serve.

Japanese Sweet Brown Rice

This very-short-grain Japanese brown rice has a little more starch than long-grain forms, so it ends up a little sticky. Its flavor is mild and lovely, and its slight stickiness makes it possible for the grains to cohere, which is useful for making rice balls. It can be found at natural food stores and Japanese markets.

Pinto Bean Soup
over rice with red chile and cheese

MAKES 10 CUPS

I always cook these beans in a pressure cooker, because they come out perfectly soft and soupy—and in only thirty minutes. If you don't have a pressure cooker, simply presoak the beans, then cook them in 2 quarts water until very soft, $1\frac{1}{2}$ hours or longer, as needed. A little masa harina, lime-treated corn flour, stirred into the soup once the beans are cooked, adds the earthy flavor of corn tortillas and thickens the liquid a tad, giving the soup a subtle body. Pour the soup over rice, add grated cheese along with other sundry garnishes, and these beans become a homey meal.

2 cups pinto beans
2 onions, finely chopped
3 garlic cloves, coarsely chopped
2 tablespoons sunflower seed or vegetable oil
3 epazote sprigs, if available, or 1 teaspoon dried
2 teaspoons dried oregano, preferably Mexican
2 teaspoons ground cumin
$\frac{1}{2}$ teaspoon ground coriander
3 New Mexican dried red chile pods, stems, seeds, and veins removed
Sea salt
3 tablespoons masa harina

Ground red chile
2 cups cooked white or brown rice
1 cup grated Cheddar or Monterey Jack cheese
2 tablespoons slivered scallion
3 tablespoons chopped cilantro
Sour cream

1. Sort through the beans, give them a rinse, and set aside while you chop the onions and garlic.

A Sonoma Zinfandel would stand up to the red chile and cheese in this soup.

2. Heat the oil in a pressure cooker and add the onions, garlic, epazote, oregano, cumin, coriander, and dried chiles. Give a stir, then add the beans along with 3 quarts water and $1\frac{1}{2}$ teaspoons salt. Fasten the lid, bring the pressure to high, then cook, maintaining the pressure for 30 minutes. Release the pressure quickly.

3. Puree 2 cups of the beans and any large pieces of chile until smooth and return them to the pot. Whisk in the masa harina and simmer for another 10 minutes. Taste for salt and heat, adding more salt or ground chile as needed. The texture should be soupy yet punctuated with beans.

4. Ladle the beans and their liquid over a mound of rice, then sprinkle on the cheese, scallion, and cilantro, ending with a dollop of sour cream.

- Add a squeeze of fresh lime juice to each bowl.
- Serve with a favorite salsa stirred in or on top.
- Definitely serve with warm corn tortillas or, a bit funkier, break some tortilla chips into the soup for some crunch.
- Serve with the masa dumplings on page 151 instead of rice.

MAKES 10 TO
12 CUPS

For beans I use
2 cups dried cranberry
beans, Madeira
(page 64), the largest
of the cranberry-type
beans, or borlotti
beans—sometimes a
mixture of odds and
ends of beans—
and cook them long
and slow. It takes no
more time to make a
lot than it does to
make a little, and you
can freeze half for
another meal.

Bean and Pasta Soup

After an intense morning of tasting everything from raw milk cheeses to giant turnips to chocolates at Slow Food's gigantic *Salone del Gusto* in Turin, I sat down to a lunch of beans and pasta. What a relief it provided from all that excitement—simple, plump beans, pasta, a little olive oil, salt. Pasta e fagioli is one of those comforting foods we need to return to on a regular basis. Beans and rice—as in red beans and rice or black-eyed peas and rice—also provide a return to culinary sanity. Instead of pasta, you could add a cup or two of cooked rice once the beans are done.

2 cups beans, such as cranberry, borlotti, or Madeira, soaked
$^{1}/_{4}$ cup extra virgin olive oil, plus extra to finish
1 onion, finely diced
$^{1}/_{4}$ cup diced carrot
$^{1}/_{4}$ cup diced celery
1 medium potato, peeled and diced
2 garlic cloves, coarsely chopped
$^{1}/_{2}$ cup chopped canned tomato
Sea salt and freshly ground pepper
$1^{1}/_{2}$ cups dried pasta, such as small macaroni, lumache, or other shapes
Minced parsley
Parmigiano-Reggiano for grating

1. Drain and rinse the beans, then set them aside.

2. Warm the oil in a wide soup pot. Add the onion, carrot, celery, potato, and garlic and cook over medium heat, stirring occasionally, for 15 to 20 minutes. Add the beans to the pot with the tomato and 10 cups water. Simmer, covered, over low heat until the beans are tender, about 2 hours. Remove a cup or so of the beans, puree them, and add them back to the soup. Season with salt and pepper.

3. Cook the pasta separately in boiling salted water until done, then add it to the soup. Serve with minced parsley, a generous drizzle of olive oil, and a grating of cheese.

Chianti Classico would be the wine choice for a soup of beans and pasta or beans and rice.

THERE ARE MANY WAYS to make black bean soup. Here are three—a lusty Cuban-inspired "made from scratch" thick soup seasoned with cumin and cilantro; a second made from canned beans with coconut milk, chile, and lime; and a traditional American pureed black bean soup seasoned with cloves and lemon. They're all different, and they're all good.

In the first recipe the beans are cooked in a pressure cooker; the second one uses canned beans; and for the third, soaked beans are cooked slowly on the stove. You can use these methods interchangeably.

Black Bean Soups

Black Bean Soup
with cumin and cilantro

MAKES 2 QUARTS

Inspired by a visit with a large and lively Cuban family in Miami, the flavors in this soup rest on "the holy trinity" of garlic, peppers, and onions. Spanish paprika provides a warm smokiness, which ham would otherwise provide. The recipe here is given for a pressure cooker and unsoaked beans. If you're not using a pressure

cooker, see page 50 for basic soaking instructions. In either case, while the beans are cooking, sauté the onion and flavorings. Combine the two and simmer to allow the flavors to develop. When bean soups sit overnight, the beans tend to drink up the liquid, so be prepared to thin it with water or stock. Should you decide to use canned beans (3 cans for this amount), be sure to cook the flavor base long enough to really soften the onions.

THE BEANS

2 cups black beans
Sea salt
3 tablespoons olive or sunflower seed oil
1 large onion, finely diced
2 small carrots, finely diced
3 celery ribs, finely diced
1 green bell pepper, finely diced
3 garlic cloves, minced
1 bunch of cilantro, stems finely sliced and leaves more roughly chopped
1 tablespoon toasted ground cumin seeds
1 teaspoon Spanish smoked paprika (page 92), or more to taste
2 bay leaves
$^{1}/_{4}$ teaspoon cayenne, or more to taste

TO FINISH

$^{1}/_{2}$ cup sour cream
Juice of $^{1}/_{2}$ lime, or more to taste

1. Rinse the beans and put them in a pressure cooker with 1½ teaspoons salt and 10 cups water. Bring the pressure to high, then maintain it for 30 minutes. Release it and let it fall by itself. Taste the beans. If they're not soft enough, simmer them until they are.

For wine, try a medium-bodied red, such as a Rioja.

2. Meanwhile, heat the oil in a medium skillet. Add the onion, carrots, celery, green pepper, garlic, and cilantro stems. Cook over medium-high heat, stirring frequently, until the onion has softened. Season with 1 teaspoon salt and add the cumin, paprika, bay leaves, and cayenne. Lower the heat and cook for 10 minutes longer, stirring occasionally and taking care not to let the paprika and cayenne burn. Add 1 cup water and continue to cook until the onion is soft, about 8 minutes.

3. Stir the onion base into the beans along with all but 3 tablespoons of the chopped cilantro leaves and cook over low heat, covered, for 20 minutes. Taste for salt.

4. Mix the sour cream, lime juice, and remaining cilantro together and season with a pinch of salt. Serve a spoonful in each bowl of soup.

MAKES ABOUT
5$\frac{1}{2}$ CUPS

Black Bean Soup
with chile, coconut milk, and lime

This soup, quickly made with canned beans, is thin enough that it can precede a meal. Or add freshly cooked rice to each bowl and let it become the meal.

2 tablespoons sunflower seed or olive oil
1 small onion, finely diced
1$\frac{1}{2}$ teaspoons toasted ground cumin seeds
1 teaspoon ground chipotle chile or minced chipotle in adobo, to taste
$\frac{1}{4}$ cup chopped cilantro, plus a little extra for garnish
Two 15$\frac{1}{2}$-ounce cans black beans, preferably organic
1 can coconut milk (about 15 ounces)
Sea salt
Juice of 1 or 2 limes, to taste

A crisp white Riesling from Alsace, an Oregon Pinot Gris, or a California Sauvignon Blanc would play off the rich coconut milk and the aromatic lime and chile.

1. Heat the oil in a wide soup pot, then add the onion, cumin, chile, and cilantro and cook over medium heat, stirring every so often, for about 5 minutes. Add $\frac{1}{2}$ cup water, lower the heat, and continue cooking until the onion is soft, about 12 minutes in all.

2. Pour in the beans plus their liquid, 2$\frac{1}{2}$ cups water, and the coconut milk. Bring to a boil and simmer for 15 minutes.

vegetable soups
60

3. Puree a cup or so of the beans and return it to the soup. Or puree all of the beans if you prefer a smooth soup. Season with salt and stir in the lime juice. Serve garnished with a pinch of chopped cilantro.

Boston-Style Black Bean Soup

Our love of chile and spice has perhaps overshadowed this wonderful old-fashioned soup, which deserves to be enjoyed as well as more contemporary versions. Enjoy it with a glass of sherry.

1$^{1}\!/_{2}$ cups black beans, soaked
3 tablespoons butter or sunflower seed oil
1 cup finely chopped onion
2 bay leaves
$^{1}\!/_{2}$ cup diced celery
2 teaspoons minced garlic
1$^{1}\!/_{2}$ teaspoons dry mustard
$^{1}\!/_{4}$ teaspoon ground cloves
Sea salt and freshly ground pepper
1 cup half-and-half, cream, or milk
4 teaspoons fresh lemon juice, or to taste
6 lemon slices, each pierced with a clove
2 tablespoons minced parsley
1 hard-cooked egg, peeled and finely diced

1. Drain and rinse the beans, then set them aside.

2. Melt the butter in a wide soup pot over medium heat, then add the onion, bay leaves, celery, and garlic. Cook, stirring occasionally, until the onion is translucent, about 5 minutes. Stir in the mustard and ground cloves, add the beans and 2 quarts water, and bring to a boil. Lower the heat, cover the pot, and simmer until the beans are partially softened, about an hour. Add 2 teaspoons salt and con-

tinue cooking until the beans are fully tender, another 30 minutes more, depending on the age of the beans.

3. Remove the soup from the heat, let it cool briefly, then puree until very smooth. Return the soup to the pot, stir in the half-and-half, and season to taste with pepper and lemon juice. Reheat to serving temperature.

4. Ladle the soup into bowls and serve with a clove-pierced lemon slice in each bowl, a sprinkling of the parsley, and diced egg on top.

With Canned Beans Use three 15-ounce cans of black beans, preferably organic. Cook the onion and spices as described in the first step, but before adding the beans add 1 cup of water and simmer until the onions are fully softened. Add the canned beans and 3½ cups of water. Cook for 15 minutes, then follow the rest of the recipe as given. Add more half-and-half or water if the soup is too thick.

MAKES ABOUT
7 CUPS

Borlotti or Madeira Bean Soup
with radicchio

I enjoy the silky-smooth pureed and strained borlotti bean soups served with shrimp in Liguria—to me a surprising but very good combination. Here the tang of the vinegar and slightly bitter radicchio make this bean soup sparkle. Unlike other stick-to-the-ribs bean-based soups, this one is thinner, the beans appearing as a garnish along with the radicchio.

THE BEANS 1¼ cups borlotti beans or Madeira beans, soaked
3 tablespoons olive oil
1 onion, diced
1 carrot, diced

1 celery rib, diced
1 bay leaf
2 garlic cloves, minced
1 tablespoon tomato paste
Chunk of Parmesan cheese rind
Sea salt and freshly ground pepper

Olive oil as needed
1 head of radicchio
Aged red wine vinegar

1. Drain and rinse the beans, then set them aside.

2. Heat the oil in a soup pot and add the onion, carrot, celery, and bay leaf. Cook over medium heat, stirring occasionally, until the onion gains some color, about 10 minutes. Add the garlic, cook for 1 minute longer, then work the tomato paste into the vegetables, letting it fry in the oil for a minute or so.

3. Add the beans, cheese rind, and 7 cups water. Bring to a boil, then lower the heat to a simmer, cover the pot, and cook for 1 hour. Add $1\frac{1}{2}$ teaspoons salt and continue cooking until the beans are fully tender, another 30 minutes or longer. Remove the bay leaf and cheese rind. Set aside a cup of the beans, puree the rest with the broth until very smooth, then return it to the pan. Taste for salt and season with pepper.

4. When you're ready to eat, generously film a cast-iron pan with olive oil. Cut the radicchio into rough $1\frac{1}{2}$-inch squares. When the oil is hot, add the radicchio to the pan, sprinkle with salt, and cook, stirring every so often, until the color turns from red to reddish brown, about 5 minutes. Add a splash of vinegar and continue cooking, stirring frequently, until the leaves are glazed and tender when you taste one. Season with a little pepper.

5. Ladle the soup into bowls, divide the reserved beans among them, then add the radicchio to each bowl.

A Barbera with good acidity would work with the depth that the Parmesan rind contributes to the soup.

hearty bean soups

Madeira Beans   One of many exotic New World beans, the Madeira is the largest of the cranberry type and, though uncommon, not impossible to find here and there. Large and mottled with purple blotches, Madeira beans can be found in specialty stores that carry assortments of exotic bean varieties and on the Internet at www.ranchogordo.com or www.phippscountry.com.

MAKES ABOUT
IO CUPS

White Bean Soup
with fried parsley and garlic

This rather straightforward soup really benefits from its finishing touch of minced parsley, sage, and garlic fried briefly in olive oil, which makes it unnecessary to add cheese, although some freshly grated Parmigiano-Reggiano would be good.

THE BEANS
2 cups white beans—Great Northern, navy, or cannellini—soaked
2 to 4 tablespoons olive oil
1 large onion, finely diced, or 1½ cups chopped leek
1 carrot, finely diced
1 celery rib, finely diced
2 large garlic cloves, smashed
Bouquet garni: a celery rib wrapped with 5 parsley branches and a thyme sprig
Chunk of Parmigiano-Reggiano cheese rind, optional
Sea salt and freshly ground pepper

TO FINISH
3 tablespoons fruity olive oil
3 tablespoons finely chopped parsley
2 tablespoons finely chopped sage
2 garlic cloves, chopped

1.   Drain and rinse the beans. Heat the oil in a wide soup pot, add the onion, carrot, and celery, and cook over medium heat, stirring occasionally, for about 5 minutes.

Add the beans, 10 cups water, the garlic, bouquet garni, and cheese rind if you're using it. Bring to a boil, then lower the heat and cook gently, covered, until the beans are soft, about an hour. Add 1½ teaspoons salt and cook until fully tender, 30 minutes longer, as needed.

2. Puree 1 to 2 cups of beans until only tiny flecks of the skins remain, then return the puree to the pot. Taste for salt and season with pepper.

3. Just before serving, heat the 3 tablespoons oil in a small skillet over medium heat. When hot (but not smoking!), throw in the parsley, sage, and garlic. Give a stir and remove from the heat. Ladle the soup into bowls, spoon the fried herbs and oil into each bowl, and season with pepper.

With this soup, drink a fruity, lighter red such as a Beaujolais, served slightly chilled, especially with the more summery versions, or a Dolcetto.

Make the soup as described. When the oil for the garnish is hot, add 2 large seeded and diced tomatoes and cook for about 30 seconds, then toss in the parsley and sage. Spoon the tomatoes into the soup and serve tepid or even chilled, with a splash of vinegar.

A Summer White Bean Soup with Parsley, Garlic, and Tomatoes

Instead of the fried herb garnish, make a pesto or basil puree (page 154) and stir it into the soup. Go ahead and add tomatoes (see preceding variation) if you like, too.

White Bean Soup with Pesto or Basil Puree

With its generous share of capers and vinegar, this salsa verde makes another lively accompaniment for beans. Make the salsa verde on page 142 and add a big spoonful to each bowl of soup.

White Bean Soup with Marjoram Salsa Verde

Spicy Chickpea and Tomato Soup
with noodles

This is one soup where using canned legumes yields a delicious soup. Your spices, however, must be fresh and potent, since old spices weaken in character.

The presence of winter squash and carrots makes for a gorgeous red-gold soup that's studded with chickpeas, seasoned with cumin, ginger, and cilantro, and finished with skinny noodles and either lentils or seasoned cooked beans called ful medames, found at Middle Eastern markets. Once, while making this soup, I added a leftover dish of lentils and roasted beets. While I'm usually cautious about adding beets to dishes, given their ability to stain, I must say that they were beautiful and good as well, so there's another idea to keep in mind.

In a perfect world I would make my own flatbread to serve alongside. Otherwise, I serve it with warmed whole wheat pita bread or naan from a bakery.

2 to 3 tablespoons olive oil, plus extra to finish
1 onion, finely diced
Pinch of saffron threads
1$\frac{1}{2}$ teaspoons paprika
1 teaspoon toasted ground cumin seeds
$\frac{1}{2}$ teaspoon ground ginger
$\frac{1}{2}$ teaspoon ground turmeric
2 carrots, sliced in rounds if small, quartered and sliced if large
1 celery rib, diced
1 heaping cup diced peeled winter squash, such as butternut
2 tablespoons *each* chopped parsley and cilantro
One 28-ounce can organic diced tomatoes with juice
One 15$\frac{1}{2}$-ounce can chickpeas, preferably organic
One 15$\frac{1}{2}$-ounce can ful medames or 1 cup cooked lentils
Sea salt and freshly ground pepper
1 cup skinny egg noodles, boiled in salted water until tender, then drained

1. Heat the oil in a wide soup pot, then add the onion, saffron, and spices. Give a stir, then cook over medium heat while you dice the vegetables, stirring the onion now and then. Add the vegetables with half the parsley and cilantro. Cook slowly until the onion is soft, another 12 to 15 minutes.

2. Add the tomatoes and their juices, the chickpeas and their juices, the ful or lentils, plus enough water to give the soup the texture you like—another 2 or 3 cups. Simmer until the carrots are cooked through, about 20 minutes. Taste for salt and season with plenty of pepper.

3. Stir in the cooked noodles, garnish with the remaining chopped parsley and cilantro, and add a few drops of olive oil to each bowl.

Chickpea and Spinach Soup
with bread crumbs

MAKES ABOUT
2 QUARTS

It does take a little more fussing to cook your own, but chickpeas basically cook themselves—you needn't hover around them. The soup may thicken as it sits, so be sure to save all the cooking liquid so that you can bring a too-thick soup back to the proper consistency without losing flavor.

As in the Provençal gratin of chickpeas and spinach, this soup unites the two with bread crumbs and an important final thread of fruity olive oil. This is one soup I make using dried chickpeas. The flavor of a long-simmered chickpea is nutty, sweet, and rich—and not at all like a canned chickpea. Plus you'll need 6 or more cups of flavorful broth, which is what you'll get if you cook your own.

THE CHICKPEAS
2 cups chickpeas, soaked
1 carrot, peeled
1 head of garlic, sliced crosswise in half
2 bay leaves
1/2 teaspoon dried oregano
Handful of parsley sprigs, tied together with string

THE SEASONINGS
Sea salt and freshly ground pepper
4 to 5 tablespoons fruity olive oil
2 onions, finely diced
1 teaspoon dried oregano, not Mexican
Good pinch of dried thyme or 1 thyme sprig

3 garlic cloves, minced
Big bunch of spinach, stems removed and leaves washed

Juice of 1 lemon, or to taste
1 cup coarse bread crumbs moistened with 1 tablespoon olive oil
Good fruity olive oil

TO FINISH

1. Drain and rinse the chickpeas and put them in a pot with the rest of the ingredients and 3 quarts water. Bring to a boil, then lower the heat, cover, and simmer until the chickpeas are tender but hold their shape. They shouldn't get quite as soft as canned chickpeas. (This can be done a day or two ahead of time.) Season with a teaspoon of salt and set aside. If you're inclined to, pinch the skins off the chickpeas and discard them.

A Provençal rosé would be a match for this Provençal mixture of spinach, chickpeas, plus the garlic, thyme, and oregano.

2. Heat the oil in a second soup pot. Add the onions, oregano, thyme, and a few pinches of salt. Cook over medium-low heat until softened, about 15 minutes, occasionally giving them a stir. Add the garlic toward the end.

3. Using a strainer, lift the cooked chickpeas into the pot with the onions and discard the rest of the aromatics. Strain the liquid and add 6 cups, setting the rest aside for the moment. Add another teaspoon of salt, then cover and simmer for 25 minutes. Puree 2 cups of the chickpeas and return them to the pot. If the soup seems too thick, thin it with any remaining liquid. Taste for salt and season with pepper.

4. Wilt the spinach in a skillet in the water clinging to its leaves, then chop and add to the chickpeas. Cook for 2 to 3 minutes, then taste again and add lemon juice to bring up the flavor. Crisp the bread crumbs in a skillet. Ladle the soup into soup plates, scatter bread crumbs over each serving, drizzle with a little additional oil, and serve.

White Bean and Black Kale Minestra
with farro

Here's a hearty soup of earthy beans, chewy grain, black kale, and tomatoes. It takes some teasing and time to cook the beans, soak the farro (page 112) so that it doesn't drink up all the stock, and spend a good 15 minutes slowly cooking the onions at the beginning, but you'll end up with the kind of soup you can happily make a meal of. It's got lots of body and doesn't need croutons, but I sometimes scatter some crispy bread crumbs on top along with a thread of olive oil and a little cheese.

THE BEANS AND
FARRO

1 cup navy, cannellini, or other white beans, soaked

Aromatics: 3 garlic cloves, peeled and crushed, a few sage leaves, a bay leaf,
    4 parsley branches

1 1/2 teaspoons sea salt

3/4 cup farro, covered with cold water for at least 1 hour

THE SOUP

2 to 4 tablespoons fruity olive oil

2 cups diced onion (1 large onion)

3/4 cup diced carrot

3/4 cup diced celery

3/4 teaspoon dried oregano

1/4 teaspoon dried thyme

2 garlic cloves, crushed and chopped

2 tablespoons tomato paste (sun-dried is good)

Splash of white or red wine or water

4 cups shredded black, Russian, or regular kale leaves

Sea salt and freshly ground pepper

One 15-ounce can organic diced tomatoes with their juice

TO FINISH

Extra virgin olive oil

Parmigiano-Reggiano for grating

1 cup bread crumbs browned in oil with minced rosemary, optional

1. Drain and rinse the beans and put them in a pot with 10 cups water and the aromatics. Bring to a boil, reduce the heat to a simmer, and cook, covered, for an hour. Add 1½ teaspoons salt and continue cooking until the beans are tender, another 30 minutes or so. Pick out the aromatics. Drain the beans and reserve the liquid.

2. Heat the oil in a wide soup pot. Add the onion, carrot, celery, herbs, and garlic. Cook over medium heat, giving the contents a stir every so often, until softened, aromatic, and golden, about 15 minutes. Stir in the tomato paste and continue cooking for 5 minutes, or until there's a glaze on the bottom of the pan, then add the wine to deglaze the pan.

3. Add the kale, the farro, drained, 1 teaspoon salt, and 1 cup water. After a few minutes, when the kale has wilted, add the tomatoes and the beans and their liquid. Bring to a boil, then reduce the heat to low, cover the pot, and simmer slowly until the farro is plump and tender, about 25 minutes.

4. Taste for salt and serve with freshly ground pepper, a spoonful of good olive oil, a grating of cheese in each bowl—and a shower of bread crumbs if you wish.

For this soup, you might drink a California Syrah or an earthy Rhône blend, such as those from Qupé or Bonny Doon.

Navy Bean and Winter Squash Soup
with sage bread crumbs

MAKES ABOUT
2 QUARTS

I alternate between using small white navy beans with the vegetables cut in a fine dice to complement their size, and using the larger cannellini beans and big chunks of vegetables. Such small differences affect the final feel of the dish—one is delicate, the other more stewlike. In either case, squash, cabbage, and turnips are all sweet vegetables, so the sizzling sage-and-garlic-infused bread crumbs are not just a garnish but an ingredient that puts everything into balance.

Should you choose
to use canned beans,
look for some of the
more unusual
varieties, such as
soldier beans, and
replace their broth
with a vegetable stock.

THE BEANS

1 cup navy or cannellini beans, soaked

3 large garlic cloves, smashed

1 onion, peeled, halved, and studded with 2 cloves

Aromatics: 1 bay leaf, several sage leaves, a thyme sprig, 4 parsley branches

1 tablespoon olive oil

Sea salt and freshly ground pepper

THE VEGETABLES

2 to 4 tablespoons olive oil

1 pound, more or less, butternut squash, peeled, seeds removed, and flesh diced

1 large onion, diced

3 to 4 small turnips (about $^3/_4$ pound), thickly peeled and cut into chunks

1 tablespoon chopped sage

2 tablespoons chopped parsley

1 plump garlic clove, chopped

Aromatics: $^1/_2$ teaspoon dried oregano, pinch of dried thyme, 2 bay leaves

$^1/_2$ pound Savoy cabbage, chopped into squares

TO FINISH

$1^1/_2$ cups fresh bread crumbs

2 tablespoons olive oil

3 tablespoons finely chopped sage

1 garlic clove, minced

For wine, a heavier
white that's good in
winter, such as a
Gewürztraminer,
which is full of spicy
flavors that contrast
with the sweetness of
the squash.

1. Drain and rinse the beans and put them in a pot with 2 quarts water, the garlic, onion, aromatics, and 1 tablespoon olive oil. Bring to a boil, then lower the heat and simmer, partially covered, for an hour. Add 1 teaspoon salt and continue cooking until the beans are tender, another half hour or so—cooking times vary according to altitude, age of beans, and hardness of water. Drain the beans, leaving them in just enough liquid so that they don't dry out, then strain and reserve the cooking water. You should have 6 to 7 cups.

2. Warm the oil in a soup pot. Add the squash, onion, turnips, sage, parsley, garlic, aromatics, and 1 teaspoon salt. Give a stir, then cook over medium heat, stirring occasionally, until the vegetables have started to brown a bit here and there and caramelize, about 15 minutes. Add the cabbage and let it wilt, then add the bean

broth or equivalent amount of vegetable stock. Bring to a boil, then lower the heat and simmer, partially covered, until the squash is tender but still intact, 15 to 20 minutes depending on size. Add the beans and continue cooking until heated through. Taste for salt and season with pepper.

3. Toss the bread crumbs with the 2 tablespoons oil and sage to moisten them, then put them in a skillet and cook slowly over medium heat until crisp and golden, about 10 minutes. Add the garlic during the last few minutes so that it doesn't burn. Season with salt and pepper. Serve the soup and add a generous helping of the hot crumbs to each bowl.

One could collect a great many traditional and appealing recipes for pea and lentil soups without much difficulty, but I've limited myself to a relative few here, only for lack of space. These legumes make the most satisfying soups and, relative to beans, in fairly short order. There's a hearty basic lentil soup with spinach (all greens are good with lentils), a luscious army-green sorrel and lentil soup (a favorite), and a lentil puree finished with a cream of pounded walnuts and garlic. One of the soups is based on red lentils, and split peas have been transformed into a light, lemony soup. Neither lentils nor peas need stock as they have a good robust flavor of their own. In fact, I often add a handful of lentils *to* a stock for just that reason.

Lots of different kinds of lentils are available to the cook today, whereas once there was just one, the German brown lentil. Now we have the tiny slate-green lentils from France, the cleverly named black Belugas, tiny Spanish pardinos, white lentils that I haven't yet used in soups, and a number of Sicilian and Italian lentils, which, like the pardinos, are very small, green-yellow-brownish, and full of flavor. (I've found similar lentils in Mexico.) Among the many split lentil and pea pulses, my favorite are the Indian red lentils, which cook quickly into a puree.

For years I shunned the dull-looking German lentils in favor of the more stylish French and Beluga types, which are handsome in salads, soups, and side dishes. But I've rediscovered them and find that I rather like their full flavor. Of course, there's nothing that says you can't mix varieties, and I often do, especially when I find myself with tail ends of various kinds. Black, slate, green, and brown lentils are as pretty as beach stones when cooked together.

On Soaking and Cooking Lentils and Peas

WHILE LENTILS AND PEAS certainly cook more quickly than beans do, I've found that it's a bit of an exaggeration to say that they can be fully cooked in twenty-five minutes. At least that's seldom true for me, which may have to do with my high altitude and hard water. In general, I find that lentils want a good forty-five minutes on the stove, unless, of course, you soak them. Another mythic quality that has made lentils and peas endearing is the notion that they don't have to be soaked. They don't, but they cook better (and more quickly) and seem to have more flavor when soaked. Let me assure you lest you become anxious about having yet something else to do that, no, you don't have to soak your lentils. But try it sometime and see what you think. It changed my cooking habits. By the way, soaking lentils was not my idea. I saw that Anne Bianchi, author of the wonderful book called *Zuppa!,* soaks her lentils, and since I admire her, I decided to give it a try. I love the results.

Lentils needn't soak overnight or even for four hours. Two hours is ideal, one hour is not bad, and failing that, letting them soak while you gather and chop your vegetables doesn't hurt. They absorb water, which not only cuts down on their cooking time but seems to open them up to absorbing and yielding more of their flavor. If you do soak your lentils (and peas), you'll find that they take less cooking liquid. I've indicated, roughly, the amounts you'll need for both soaked and unsoaked legumes in each recipe.

A Rustic Lentil Soup
with spinach

All greens are good with lentils, and I especially like to add them to a soup that's going to be a meal. That way you get all your good foods together in one bowl.

As this makes a generous amount, you may have leftovers, so take a look at the suggestions following the recipe for ways to serve this soup.

1$\frac{1}{2}$ cups brown or mixed lentils, soaked if possible

2 to 4 tablespoons olive oil, plus extra for serving

1 large onion, finely diced

1 carrot, grated or finely diced

1 red bell pepper, roasted, peeled, and chopped, or 1 bottled roasted pepper, chopped

2 tablespoons chopped parsley

2 garlic cloves, chopped

2 tablespoons tomato paste

1 tablespoon prepared mustard

$\frac{1}{2}$ cup dry red wine

1 bay leaf

6 to 8 cups water, Vegetable Stock (page 13), or chicken stock, as needed

Sea salt and freshly ground pepper

Hefty bunch of spinach, stems removed, leaves washed and chopped

Chopped mint or parsley for garnish

Red wine vinegar to taste

1. If you haven't soaked them, cover the lentils with hot water and set them aside while you start the rest of the soup.

2. Warm the oil in a wide soup pot. Add the onion, carrot, red pepper, and parsley. Cook over medium heat, stirring now and then, until the onion is softened and starting to color, about 10 minutes. Add the garlic, then stir in the tomato paste and mustard, working both into the vegetables and cooking until there's a film on the bottom of the pot. Pour in the wine, scrape up the pan juices, then simmer

A California Pinot Noir, one with bright fruit and earthiness from the Russian River Valley, would be a good choice for this robust soup.

until partially reduced after a few minutes. Drain the lentils and add them to the pot with the bay leaf and water, using the larger amount if the lentils were soaked only briefly. Bring to a boil, then reduce the heat to a simmer, cover the pan, and cook for 30 minutes. Add 1½ teaspoons salt and continue cooking until the lentils are soft, another 10 to 20 minutes. Taste for salt and season with pepper.

3. Add the spinach to the soup and cook until wilted, about 2 minutes. Taste the soup and add the mint and a little vinegar to sharpen the flavors.

Four Serving Ideas
- Shave thin slices of Parmigiano-Reggiano or Asiago cheese over the soup before serving.
- Peel, seed, and dice one or two tomatoes—there may still be some around in late fall—and stir them into the hot soup at the end.
- Add a cup or so of cooked pasta to the soup just before serving. The pasta may be tiny shapes like orzo or stars or bigger pieces, such as little shells or snails.
- Puree the lentils until very smooth, then add the spinach and any of the garnishes suggested above.

MAKES A GENEROUS
2 QUARTS

Lentil Soup
with cumin, cilantro, and chard

A lentil soup for any season, this potage is brightened with a final addition of cilantro and chard. A spoonful of yogurt brightens the soup even more—and completes the protein while doing so. I like to use a mixture of lentils—slate-green French ones, German brown, and black Belugas—all soaked together for an hour or more if time allows. They make a more visually interesting soup, and mixing and matching gives you a way to use up those odds and ends of lentils that accumulate in the cupboard.

1¼ cups lentils (brown, green, black, or a mixture), soaked for 1 hour or longer

2 large garlic cloves, pounded with 1 teaspoon salt

Sea salt and freshly ground pepper

2 bay leaves

4 parsley branches and 4 cilantro branches, tied together

2 to 4 tablespoons olive or sunflower seed oil

1 large onion, finely diced

1 teaspoon ground cumin

6 chard leaves, finely chopped (about 4 cups)

¼ to ½ cup finely chopped cilantro

Yogurt, about 1 tablespoon per serving, or lemon juice to taste

If it's more convenient, you can cook the lentils and onions a day or two before, then add the chard and cilantro just before you serve the soup.

1. Drain the lentils. Put them in a soup pot with 5 cups water (7 if they haven't been soaked), the garlic, 1 teaspoon salt, the bay leaves, and the parsley and cilantro bundle. Bring to a boil, then lower the heat and simmer, covered, until tender, about 25 minutes for the soaked lentils, 45 minutes if not soaked. Taste to be sure. Remove the bay leaves and herb bundle.

2. Once the lentils are cooking, heat the oil in a medium skillet. Add the onion and cumin and cook over medium heat, stirring frequently, until it starts to brown, 15 to 20 minutes. Add to the simmering lentils.

3. When you're ready to serve, simmer the chard in a little water until soft, 8 to 10 minutes. Add it with any juices to the soup along with the chopped cilantro. Taste for salt and season with pepper. Serve with a spoonful of yogurt in each bowl. Or, if you're not using yogurt, squeeze a little lemon juice into the soup before serving to bring up the acidity and brighten the flavors.

For wine, we suggest an assertive white wine, such as an Albariño or a Rioja Bianco from Spain, one that can stand up to the cilantro and chard.

lentil and pea soups

Cream of Lentil-Sorrel Soup

This soup is a luminous iron-green puree, tart from the sorrel, thick enough to be substantial, and smooth from the cream. An altogether delicious soup, it's one to enjoy in the spring or fall when sorrel abounds and it's cool enough for lentils to be appealing. As with any pureed soup, it needs something for texture, and here it's buttered toast served on the side or broken into each bowl.

I use brown lentils or pardinos here as their skins break down easily. I also soak them or cook them longer than usual so that they'll puree easily. Whirl the soup in a blender at high speed so that the skins are entirely pulverized. Then, for a really silky soup, pass it through a food mill with a fine screen.

1 cup brown lentils or pardinos, soaked for at least 1 hour

2 to 4 tablespoons fruity olive oil

1 onion, sliced

2 celery ribs, sliced

1 carrot, sliced

2 bay leaves

Handful of parsley, chopped (about $\frac{1}{2}$ cup)

3 garlic cloves, chopped

6 to 8 cups water, Vegetable Stock (page 13), or chicken stock

Sea salt and freshly ground pepper

2 packed cups ribbed sorrel leaves (about $3\frac{1}{2}$ ounces), a few leaves set aside

$\frac{1}{2}$ cup cream or 1 cup half-and-half

TO FINISH

Buttered toast for each serving

Several tablespoons cream or crème fraîche

Try an unoaked Napa Valley Sauvignon Blanc with the earthy lentils and tart sorrel.

1. If you haven't soaked them, rinse the lentils, cover them with hot water, and set them aside while you prepare everything else. When you're ready to start cooking, drain them.

2. Heat the oil in a soup pot and add the vegetables, bay leaves, parsley, and garlic. Give a stir, then cook over medium-high heat, stirring now and then, for 5 min-

utes. Add the lentils, water or stock, and 1½ teaspoons salt. Bring to a boil, then simmer, covered, until the lentils are squishy-soft, as long as an hour.

3. Remove the bay leaves. Add the sorrel and allow it to melt into the hot liquid, about 3 minutes, then puree the soup in a blender on high speed. Pass everything through the finest holes of a food mill, if desired. Stir in the cream, taste for salt, and season with pepper.

4. Break the toast into small pieces. Drizzle a teaspoon of cream or crème fraîche, beaten first with a fork until smooth, into each bowl of soup. Snip the reserved sorrel into fine slivers over the top, add the croutons, and serve.

Lentil Soup
with pounded walnuts and cream

MAKES 2 QUARTS

While I've certainly used walnuts in a lentil salad, I never paired them in a soup until I encountered this recipe in Anne Bianchi's book *Zuppa!* Pounded into a paste with garlic and cream, they turn a humble legume into a soup that is both elegant and robust. Nothing more than a bright little chicory salad is needed to finish the meal.

Although a vegetable stock (try the Roasted Vegetable Stock on page 15) and even water would be fine here, chicken or turkey stock makes a much fuller and richer-tasting soup. Regardless of what you use, you will be happier with your soup if you soak the lentils first. The liquid measurement given here is for lentils that have been soaked. If you skip that step, plan on using as much as 2 cups extra liquid.

2 cups lentils, soaked for 1 to 2 hours
2 to 4 tablespoons butter

THE LENTILS

1 onion, finely diced
1 bay leaf
6 cups water, Vegetable Stock, or chicken or turkey stock
Sea salt and freshly ground pepper

THE WALNUTS

1 plump garlic clove
⅓ cup walnuts, lightly toasted unless freshly cracked
½ cup cream or crème fraîche
Minced parsley to finish

Staying in the region of the Piedmont where this soup originated, we suggest an unoaked white wine, such as an Arneis.

1. Drain the lentils if you've soaked them. Melt the butter in a soup pot, add the onion and bay leaf, and cook over medium-high heat for 5 minutes, stirring now and then.

2. Add the lentils and the liquid (7 to 8 cups, if the lentils have not been soaked) along with 1 teaspoon salt. Bring to a boil, then simmer, covered, for about 30 minutes, or until the lentils are completely soft. Taste for salt and season with pepper.

3. Pound the garlic in a mortar with a pinch of salt, then add the walnuts and start working them into a paste. Add cream a teaspoon or so at a time, which will make it easier to break down the nuts. Any extra cream can go directly into the finished soup.

4. Serve the soup in soup plates and add a good spoonful of the walnut cream to each. Sprinkle a little parsley over each serving, add a grinding of pepper, and enjoy.

Three Variations

- Since the pounded nuts always make me think of those delicious Ligurian pasta dishes with pounded walnuts, I sometimes vary the soup by adding cooked broken pasta.
- The parsley truly brightens everything—but other herbs that are good here are marjoram, basil, and tarragon.
- Sorrel is good, too, either sliced into short ribbons and stirred into the hot soup or cooked, pureed, and stirred into the lentils.

Lentil and Chestnut Soup
with fennel

Rather than being dense and creamy as many chestnut soups are, this one is studded with chunks of fennel-seasoned chestnuts. The sweetness of the chestnuts and the pronounced flavor of the fennel conspire to make an unusual and beguiling soup. A welcome note of acidity comes from the wine and tomato.

If you can get fresh chestnuts that have been kept damp and cool rather than treated as nuts and dried, use them. Otherwise, turn to canned chestnuts. A ten-ounce can will be plenty. For lentils I'm partial to the French "blondes," pardinos, and other small, golden-green lentils. But lacking them, German browns, greens from Le Puy, or the two mixed together work well.

1 cup lentils, soaked for 1 to 2 hours if possible

1 tablespoon olive oil
1/3 to 1/2 cup *each* diced carrot and celery
1 small onion, finely diced
1 small fennel bulb, stalks removed and the rest finely diced
1 garlic clove, minced
Aromatics: 1 bay leaf, a thyme sprig, 1/2 teaspoon dried oregano, pinch of fennel seeds
2 tablespoons finely chopped celery leaves
Sea salt and freshly ground pepper

One 10-ounce can chestnuts, drained and coarsely chopped, or 1 pound fresh chestnuts

3 tablespoons olive oil, plus extra to finish
1 teaspoon oregano leaves
1/2 teaspoon fennel seeds, crushed
1/4 teaspoon dried thyme
1 tablespoon tomato paste
1/2 cup dry white wine
6 long slices French or Italian country bread, toasted and brushed with olive oil
Minced celery leaves or parsley for garnish

Lentil and Chestnut Soup
with Fennel

1. Drain the lentils if you soaked them. If you didn't, cover them with hot water and set aside. Warm the olive oil in a soup pot and add the carrot, celery, onion, fennel, garlic, aromatics, and celery leaves. Add a teaspoon of salt and cook over medium-low heat for about 5 minutes. Drain the lentils, if need be, add them to the pot along with 1 quart water (6 cups if they weren't soaked), and bring to a boil. Reduce the heat and simmer, covered, until the lentils are tender, 20 to 40 minutes, depending on whether they were soaked. Remove the bay leaf, taste for salt, and season with a little pepper.

2. Prepare the chestnuts while the lentils are cooking. If fresh, cut an × with a paring knife into the flat sides of the chestnuts. Put them in a saucepan, cover with water, and boil gently until the peels can be pulled off, about 20 minutes. Remove them one at a time from the water and peel while they're hot so that you can remove the brown skin that clings to the seed. Whether fresh or canned, dice them into small chunks.

3. Warm the 3 tablespoons of oil in a skillet. Add the chopped chestnuts, oregano, fennel seeds, and thyme. Cook over medium-low heat for several minutes, then work in the tomato paste and add the wine. Reduce the heat to low and cook, stirring only a few times, for about 5 minutes. Add this to the soup when the lentils are done. Taste for salt and season with pepper. Serve with long croutons broken into the soup, a drizzle of olive oil, and minced celery leaves or parsley.

A simple, medium-bodied red wine, such as a Côtes-du-Rhône, has the spice and fruit to make a match with the chestnuts and fennel.

Red Lentil and Colorful Vegetable Soup

MAKES A SCANT
2 QUARTS

Here's a light, vegetable-rich soup that's pretty, aromatic, and nearly effortless to make. Butter provides the richness that's needed in such a simple soup, but you can use a warm-tasting oil, such as sunflower seed oil, if you prefer. Cut everything rather fine—$\frac{1}{4}$- to $\frac{1}{3}$-inch dice—about the same size as the lentils or a bit larger.

2 to 4 tablespoons butter or sunflower seed oil

1 large onion, finely diced

1 long celery rib, peeled and diced

4 skinny long carrots, finely diced or cut into rounds (about 1 cup)

1 cup finely diced peeled winter squash or zucchini

3 tablespoons minced cilantro stems

Sea salt and freshly ground pepper

1 teaspoon ground turmeric

$\frac{1}{2}$ teaspoon ground cumin

1 cup diced fresh or canned tomatoes with their juice

1 cup red lentils, rinsed well

Juice of 1 lime, or to taste

4 scallions, including an inch of the greens, sliced

To drink, try a Pinot Blanc or a Riesling from Alsace or Washington State.

1. Melt half the butter in a wide soup pot. Add the onion and cook over medium heat, stirring occasionally, while you dice the celery, carrots, and squash, and mince the cilantro stems. Add them to the onion, sprinkle on 1½ teaspoons salt, the turmeric, and the cumin, and cook for 5 minutes.

2. Add the tomato, lentils, and 5½ cups water. Bring to a boil, then lower the heat and simmer, partially covered, until the lentils have softened, 20 to 30 minutes. Taste for salt and add several grindings of pepper. Season with lime juice.

3. Melt the remaining butter in a small skillet, add the scallions, and toss over high heat to wilt them, about 2 minutes. Serve the soup with some of the scallions in each bowl and/or any of the finishing touches suggested below.

Three Finishing Touches

- Toast or fry triangles of pita bread in olive oil until crisp, then add one or two pieces to each bowl.
- Serve with a spoonful of basmati rice or a rice timbale in the bowl. In summer, include diced yellow or orange tomatoes as well as the other vegetables.
- Add a dollop of yogurt to the soup as you serve it—with or without either of the other two garnishes.

Yellow Pea and Coconut Milk Soup
with spinach, rice, and spiced yogurt

This soup starts out thin, but when the spinach and rice are added it ends up with layers of textures and colors. For a lighter first-course soup, omit the rice or use very little.

Split peas take at least an hour to cook, which is one good reason to soak them for a couple of hours, unless you pop them into a pressure cooker for twenty-five minutes on high. Another alternative is to use red lentils, which break down quickly into a light, golden soup.

THE PEAS

2 cups yellow split peas, rinsed and soaked for at least 1 hour if possible
2 bay leaves
3 cloves
Sea salt and freshly ground pepper
2 to 4 tablespoons butter, light sesame oil, or a mixture
1 large onion, finely chopped
$^1\!/_4$ cup minced cilantro stems
$1^1\!/_2$ teaspoons ground turmeric
1 teaspoon ground cardamom
$^1\!/_2$ teaspoon ground cinnamon
Pinch of hot red pepper flakes
One 15-ounce can coconut milk
Juice of 1 large lime, or to taste
3 tablespoons chopped cilantro

TO FINISH

$^1\!/_2$ cup rice
$^1\!/_2$ teaspoon *each* ground turmeric and paprika
$^1\!/_4$ teaspoon *each* cumin seeds and freshly ground pepper
$^1\!/_2$ cup yogurt
Large bunch of spinach, stems removed, well washed

1. If you've soaked the peas, drain and put them in a pot with 2 quarts water, the bay leaves, cloves, and $1^1\!/_2$ teaspoons salt. Bring to a boil, then lower the heat to a simmer and cook, partially covered, while you go on to the next step.

An Oregon Pinot Gris
or one from Alsace will
have the weight that
complements this soup's
layers of flavors.

2. Melt the butter in a medium skillet over medium heat, then add the onion and cilantro stems. Cook, stirring frequently, until the onion starts to color and soften, about 10 minutes. Add the spices and $\frac{1}{2}$ cup water from the simmering peas, and cook until the water has cooked away. Add the onion to the simmering peas and continue cooking until both are very soft, about an hour in all. Remove the bay leaves and cloves, then puree. Return the soup to the stove and stir in the coconut milk. Add the lime juice, then taste for salt and season with pepper. Stir in the chopped cilantro.

3. To finish, bring 1 cup water to a boil, then add $\frac{1}{4}$ teaspoon salt and the rice. Give it a stir, lower the heat, and cover the pan. Cook until the rice has absorbed the water and is done, about 15 minutes. Combine the spices with the yogurt and set aside. In a separate skillet, wilt the spinach in the water clinging to its leaves, then chop it coarsely. To serve, ladle the soup into bowls, divide the spinach leaves among them, then add cooked rice to each bowl and serve with a spoonful of the spiced yogurt.

MAKES ABOUT
2 QUARTS

Cream of Split and Fresh Pea Soup
with rosemary and lemon

My neighbors gave this soup high marks. Fresh or frozen green peas and lemon make a light, lemony split pea soup that can be made in minutes if you use a pressure cooker, in about an hour if not. As with lentils, split peas benefit from a preliminary soaking in water, if not for a whole hour (or two), then at least while you gather your ingredients and begin making the soup.

1 cup green split peas, rinsed and soaked for 1 to 2 hours if possible
2 tablespoons olive oil
1 tablespoon butter
1 large onion, diced

2 carrots, diced

1 large celery rib, including any pale leaves, diced

2 tablespoons chopped rosemary

2 tablespoons chopped parsley

2 bay leaves

2 garlic cloves, chopped

Sea salt and freshly ground pepper

$^{1}/_{2}$ teaspoon Spanish smoked paprika (page 92), or more to taste

2 cups shelled fresh or frozen peas

1 cup half-and-half or light cream

Zest and juice of 1 lemon

2 tablespoons butter or oil for frying

1 cup small bread cubes

1. If you haven't soaked them, cover the peas with hot water and set them aside while you chop the vegetables and cook the onion. Then drain them.

To drink, choose an herbaceous white, such as a Sauvignon Blanc from Sonoma's Russian River.

2. Heat the oil and 1 tablespoon butter in a soup pot over medium heat. Add the onion, carrots, celery, half of the rosemary, the parsley, and the bay leaves. Cook, stirring occasionally, for 15 minutes, or until the vegetables are browned. Add the garlic, $1^{1}/_{2}$ teaspoons salt, and the smoked paprika and cook for a few minutes more.

3. Add the split peas and 6 cups water. Stir frequently until the water comes to a boil, then lower the heat and simmer, covered, until the peas have completely broken down, 1 hour or more. (Or cook in a pressure cooker on high for 20 minutes, then release quickly.) Add the fresh or frozen peas, cook for 2 minutes more, then puree the soup in batches with the half-and-half until smooth. Return the soup to the pot. Add half the remaining rosemary and the lemon zest and return the pot to the heat. Bring up the flavor further by seasoning with salt, lemon juice, pepper, and more smoked paprika, all to taste.

4. Melt the 2 tablespoons butter in a small saucepan, add the bread, and toss over medium-low heat until lightly browned and crisp, 6 to 8 minutes. Add the rest of

the rosemary and a pinch of salt and squeeze in the last few drops of lemon juice. Continue cooking until crisp again, another 1 or 2 minutes. Scatter the croutons over the soup and serve.

Smoked Paprika   Spanish smoked paprika (pimentón de la Vera) is rich brick red and smoky. While delicious in its own right (try it over fried eggs or in mashed potatoes), it's a boon to those cooks who want to get that element of smoke into a dish when bacon isn't an option. In the past I've used chipotle chiles to do the same, but they're so hot that they simply take over. Spanish paprika is much better, plus it comes in both sweet and hot forms, so you can have the heat if you like. In this book I've used the sweet pimentón de la Vera. It can be found in gourmet food stores or online at tienda.com or penzeys.com.

Black-Eyed Peas
with mustard greens and rice

A homey Sunday-night sort of soup that makes no pretensions to being hoppin'
John or any other southern dish but simply a bowl of delicious nourishment. I've
found that frozen black-eyed peas take as long to cook as dried ones that have
been soaked—a good hour and a half. Brown butter mixed with roasted sesame
oil has a vaguely meaty flavor, which isn't detectable as either butter or sesame.
And once again, the smoked Spanish paprika (page 92) stands in for the smoky
flavor of bacon or ham.

2 tablespoons butter

1 tablespoon roasted sesame oil

2 medium onions, finely diced

3 bay leaves

2 celery ribs, diced

2 garlic cloves, chopped

1 teaspoon dried thyme

1 small dried cayenne pepper or chile de árbol or $\frac{1}{2}$ teaspoon hot red pepper
    flakes

1 teaspoon Spanish smoked paprika

1 teaspoon toasted ground cumin

Few tablespoons chopped celery leaves

1 tablespoon tomato paste

1 pound (2 cups) frozen black-eyed peas or 1 cup dried, soaked overnight

Sea salt and freshly ground pepper

1 bunch of mustard greens

1 cup cooked brown or white rice

Hot sauce for serving

TO FINISH

1. Melt the butter in a wide soup pot over medium heat and let it brown for several
   minutes until it smells nutty. Add the sesame oil, then the onions, bay leaves, celery, garlic, thyme, chile, smoked paprika, cumin, and celery leaves. Cook, stirring
   occasionally, until the onions have browned, about 20 minutes. Stir in the tomato

A spicy, fruity red, such
as a Spanish Rioja or a
California Zinfandel,
can take on the
mustard greens.

paste, then add the beans (drain them first if you used dried), 2 quarts water, and 1 teaspoon salt. Simmer, covered, until the beans are tender. Taste for salt and season with pepper.

2. Cut the mustard greens off their stems and wash them. Simmer in salted water to cover until tender, a few minutes, then transfer to a strainer, rinse with cool water, and chop. Stir them into the beans. Taste once more for salt and season with plenty of pepper. Add a few spoonfuls of rice to each bowl and serve with Tabasco, Crystal, or other favorite hot sauce on the side.

MAKES ABOUT
7 CUPS

Peanut Soup,
Senegalese style

Although I'm a devoted make-it-from scratch kind of cook, it's great to have a few soups in your repertoire that go together as easily as this one does and make as impressive a last-minute supper. A gorgeous thick reddish soup, it is truly a meal in a bowl and a smallish bowl at that—this amount will serve six to eight. I sometimes thin it with water or tomato juice and add cooked rice to the bowl, and leftovers have made a succulent topping for seared tofu. I've made a number of peanut soups in my life, but this one, which comes, with some variations, from James Peterson's big book *Splendid Soups,* is my favorite. Using roasted peanut oil (page 24) only adds to the overall flavor.

THE SOUP

1 to 2 tablespoons roasted peanut oil
1 large onion, cut into ½-inch dice
1 large garlic clove, minced
¼ cup chopped cilantro stems
¼ to ½ teaspoon cayenne or hot red pepper flakes, to taste
2 tablespoons curry powder
One 28-ounce can crushed tomatoes

⅔ cup peanut butter, preferably organic and unsweetened

1 cup coconut milk, or more to taste

Sea salt

2 tablespoons chopped cilantro, plus whole branches for garnish

Yogurt

Lime wedges

1. Heat the oil in a soup pot, then add the onion, garlic, and cilantro stems. Give a stir, then cook over high heat for a few minutes to warm the onion. Lower the heat to medium and cook until the onion has softened somewhat, 10 to 12 minutes. Stir in the cayenne and curry powder.

For this lively soup, consider a medium-bodied bright, fruity white wine, such as an Alsatian Pinot Gris.

2. Add 3 cups water and the tomatoes, including all their juices. Stir well and bring to a boil. Drop in the peanut butter and simmer until the onions are soft and the peanut butter has dissolved, about 15 minutes. Stir in the coconut milk. Season the soup with salt. It will take less than most soups.

3. Just before serving, add the chopped cilantro. Serve with a dollop of yogurt in each bowl and a wedge of lime on the side.

4 SOUPS BASED ON BREAD AND GRAINS

*I*find those primitive soups that depend on stale bread and grains rather appealing, especially as we have very good bread these days. And since we don't always finish one loaf before it's replaced with a new one, it's good to know that a panade, or bread-thickened soup, provides a great place to use up pieces of a wholesome, good-tasting loaf.

Grain-based soups have the virtue of making affordable soups that are at once filling and soothing, if not downright comforting. Some, such as rice cooked in milk or barley with sour cream, are great foods for young children or adults a bit off their feed. But some can be light and lively, such as quinoa, usually recognized in a salad or as a side dish, or robust, distinct grains of true wild rice (page 117) paired with celery. Often grain-based soups are paired with chickpeas or beans, but I've kept them in this chapter because it's the grain that predominates rather than the bean.

Bread- and grain-based soups have a long history. They tend to be born out of poverty and can be as minimal as bread (or grain) simmered in water or perhaps a little milk. We can make them better than that today, and we do. In fact, we have something of a love affair with some bread-based soups, such as *pappa al pomodoro*, Italy's famous bread and tomato soup, or *soupe à l'oignon gratinée* with its lid of toast and cheese. Soups based on farro (page 112), the "new" ancient grain, have a certain cachet, and you may be familiar with wild rice chowder if you've eaten in Minnesota. Soups simply give us another way in which to enjoy these nourishing foods.

SERVES 1 AS A
MAIN DISH

Bread and Cabbage Soup
with Gorgonzola cheese

Sounds pretty drab, doesn't it? It's not. Here we have the pretty green cabbage soup from Chapter 8 (minus the sour cream), simmered with torn pieces of country-style bread. Not unlike a *pappa al pomodoro,* it's a rustic soup to be sure and one I believe you'll return to. This is a great way to serve any leftover cabbage and potato soup—or simply do it this way from the start.

2 cups Green Cabbage Soup with Potatoes and Sour Cream (page 203)
1 slice rustic whole wheat bread, slightly stale or toasted
1 slice Gorgonzola or other blue cheese, such as Point Reyes or Maytag blue

The Gorgonzola wants a bright red wine with good acidity, such as a Barbera or Dolcetto.

Heat the soup. Tear the bread into small pieces and add it to the pot. Cover, turn off the heat, and let stand for 10 minutes. Ladle into a soup plate, place the Gorgonzola on top, and serve. Break up the bread as you eat the soup.

Rustic Bread and Tomato Soup

MAKES ABOUT
8 CUPS

This recipe serves
four, but should you
want to make this for
more or fewer people,
use this formula: per
person, plan on
1 pound (or 1 cup
diced) tomato, 1 cup
broth, and 1 slice of
bread.

Although I've made plenty of panades of tomatoes and bread—especially in the company of wild mushrooms—I'm a latecomer to *pappa al pomodoro*. My loss, for this is an exceptional soup, as so many know. It's something of a glorified tomato sauce thickened with day-old bread that drinks up the juices and gives a soothing texture to what is, in the end, a thick but light soup.

While a bread and tomato soup might well celebrate the season's best tomatoes, it can also be made with canned ones.

There are two approaches you can take to making a bread and tomato soup. One is to make a vegetable stock emphasizing summer vegetables and use that for the liquid. The other is to forgo the stock but create a base of flavor with those basic stock elements—carrots, celery, and onion. Since the stock method lets me use the extra summer vegetables I'm bound to have on hand, I prefer to use it. Otherwise, in step 3 I would add to the diced onion ¾ cup *each* diced carrot and celery and forgo the stock.

1 quart vegetable stock made with summer vegetables (page 10) or water
Tomato paste as needed
4 cups peeled, seeded, and diced tomatoes, fresh or canned (4 pounds fresh)
3 garlic cloves
Leaves from 8 parsley sprigs
Big handful of basil leaves
3 tablespoons olive oil, plus extra to finish
1 large red onion, finely diced
Sea salt and freshly ground pepper
1 teaspoon sugar, if needed
4 thick slices stale sturdy bread, crusts removed and bread torn or cut into pieces
Cubes of young Asiago cheese or grated aged Asiago or Parmigiano-Reggiano, optional

1. If you're using stock, add a few teaspoons of tomato paste to it. Simmer, covered, for 30 minutes.

2. While the stock is cooking, score the blossom end of the tomatoes, dip them for 10 to 15 seconds into boiling water, then put them into a bowl of cool water. Remove the skins and add them to the simmering stock. Halve the tomatoes and squeeze the seeds and juices through a strainer. Add the seeds to the stock along with the tomato cores. Dice the tomatoes. Mince the garlic with the parsley and basil. When the stock has simmered for 30 minutes, strain it.

3. Warm the olive oil in a wide soup pot. Add the onion, give it a stir, and cook, stirring occasionally, until softened and starting to color, 8 to 10 minutes. Add the herb and garlic mixture, followed by the tomatoes. Season with 1 teaspoon salt and add the stock. Bring to a boil, then lower the heat and simmer, covered, for 15 minutes. Taste the soup. If it seems a little thin, stir in a teaspoon or two of tomato paste to concentrate the flavor. If the soup seems tart, add the sugar.

4. Add the bread and simmer for 5 minutes more, giving it a chance to absorb the juices and break down. Serve the soup with olive oil laced over the top, freshly ground black pepper, and the cheese if desired.

A Sangiovese-based wine, clearly Chianti, would be the wine to serve with this Tuscan soup.

Onion Panade
with olives and lemon

SERVES 4 TO 6

I find it's very difficult to make a good onion soup without the benefit of dark, salty beef stock to balance the vegetable's natural sweetness. But this panade, a "soup" so thick that it's served with a spoon not a ladle, made with juicy Texas 1015s, the first fresh onions of the season, lemon zest, and olives, works. It's the olives and lemon that do the trick.

A panade takes a while to put together since the onions need forty-five minutes on the stove, then the whole dish takes another forty-five minutes in the oven, so it's not one to undertake at six if you want to eat much before eight. However, you can cook the onions ahead of time, toast the bread while the oven is warming, then put the dish together and bake it. Use water for the liquid or make a light vegetable stock while the onions are cooking.

6 to 8 onions (2½ to 3 pounds), halved and thinly sliced
3 tablespoons fruity Provençal olive oil
Sea salt and freshly ground pepper
1 large thyme sprig or a pinch of thyme
1 bay leaf
4 long strips lemon peel, about ½ inch wide
1 cup white or red wine
2 teaspoons tomato paste
⅓ cup pitted Niçoise olives
3 cups Herb and Garlic Broth (page 43), White Bean Broth (page 36), or water
½ pound sliced slightly stale sourdough or levain bread
1 garlic clove, halved lengthwise
½ cup freshly grated Parmigiano-Reggiano
½ cup crumbled goat cheese, such as Bûcheron, optional

The ingredients in this panade strongly suggest a Provençal rosé, such as Bandol, for wine.

1. Using a wide pot or skillet, cook the onions in 2 tablespoons of the oil with ½ teaspoon salt, the thyme, bay leaf, and lemon peel, covered, over medium-low heat. Give them a stir every now and then, but don't expect them to sizzle or brown—new onions will give off a lot of juice, which here only adds to the dish. Once they are meltingly soft, after about 35 minutes, add the wine, tomato paste, and olives. Cook for 10 minutes, then add the broth and simmer for 10 minutes more. Taste for salt and season with pepper.

2. While the onions are cooking, preheat the oven to 375°F. Brush the bread with the remaining tablespoon of olive oil, set it on a sheet pan, and bake until crisp and golden, about 10 minutes. Remove and rub each piece with the garlic.

3. Lightly oil a gratin dish. Break half the bread into pieces and scatter them over the bottom. Using a slotted spoon, cover the bread generously with the onions and scatter with half the grated cheese. There's no need to remove the lemon—by the

time it's cooked it will be very soft and delicious. Add the crumbles of goat cheese as well, if you're using it. Add the remaining bread, cover with the rest of the onions, and pour over the broth. Cover with the remaining cheese, set the dish on the sheet pan if it's very full, and bake until the top has formed a golden, bubbling surface, about 45 minutes. Let settle for a few minutes before serving.

A Really Good Mushroom Soup
thickened with bread

This is my new company soup. While it will be good made with water, if you make it with Hearty Mushroom Broth, even 2 or 3 cups of it, or Mushroom Stock, you will have a truly spectacular soup in about 20 minutes. A piece of bread or a cup of bread crumbs gives it just enough body, eliminating the need to make a roux. And while I seldom make anything with cream, this soup is one exception. A generous splash really brings all the good flavors together.

A joy to make and a pleasure to view—it's all pebbly with its swirls of cream and black pepper—it doesn't need an herb or a garnish, although I do like to sauté a couple of mushrooms and add them at the end. Good hot in winter or chilled in summer.

2 or 3 tablespoons butter

½ cup chopped shallot or onion

2 tablespoons chopped parsley

1 pound mushrooms, rinsed and chopped

Sea salt and freshly ground pepper

1 garlic clove, chopped

1 slice firm-textured bread or 1 cup bread crumbs

1 quart Hearty Mushroom Broth (page 34), Mushroom Stock (page 14), or stock
    plus water

½ to ¾ cup cream

A California
Chardonnay from Los
Carneros goes well
with both the cream in
the soup and the
earthiness of the
mushrooms.

1. Melt 2 tablespoons butter in a wide soup pot over medium-high heat. When it foams, add the shallot and parsley, cook for several minutes, then add the mushrooms and stir to coat with the butter. Season with ½ teaspoon salt. Cook over medium heat until the mushrooms' liquid is released, after several minutes, then add the garlic, bread, and stock. Bring to a boil and simmer, covered, for 15 minutes.

2. Puree the soup in a blender, leaving it a bit textured with flecks of mushroom, and then return the soup to the pan. Taste for salt. Swirl the cream into the soup with a spoon, and season with pepper.

MAKES 10 CUPS

Barley Soup
with red beans, corn, and sage

You can make this soup using canned beans or home-cooked Madeira (page 64) or borlotti beans, my beans of choice. Red kidney beans are on the sweet side but also usable. With the addition of the last of the season's corn, you'll have a soup that's made for the first cool days of fall.

Barley is a *thirsty, thirsty* grain. It can drink up to around four times its volume in water—or the soup liquid—so I strongly suggest a two-hour soak before cooking so that you end up with soup rather than a barley dish. Of course you can always thin a thickened soup with water, but flavor is lost when you do that. If you don't have time for a soak, at least cover your barley with hot water while you prep everything to give it a head start.

1 cup barley, soaked in cold water for 2 hours
2 tablespoons butter
1 tablespoon olive oil
2 bay leaves
10 large sage leaves, chopped, or about 2 teaspoons dried

1 large red onion, finely diced

½ cup or more diced carrot

1 or 2 large garlic cloves, chopped (about 2 teaspoons)

3 tablespoons chopped parsley, plus extra minced parsley for garnish

1 teaspoon tomato paste

Sea salt and freshly ground pepper

2 ears corn

One 15-ounce can borlotti or red kidney beans or 1½ cups cooked borlotti or
 Madeira beans

1. If you haven't soaked it, cover the barley with hot water before you start prepping the soup vegetables.

2. Melt the butter with the oil, bay leaves, and sage in a wide soup pot. Add the onion and carrot, stir, and cook over medium heat, stirring occasionally, for about 10 minutes, until the onion begins to take on some color. Add the garlic and chopped parsley, then work in the tomato paste.

3. Drain the barley; add it to the pot with 2 quarts water (or stock) and 1½ teaspoons salt. Bring to a boil, reduce the heat to simmer, then cover and cook until the barley is tender, about 35 minutes. Taste for salt and season with pepper.

4. Meanwhile, shuck the corn and slice off the top halves of the kernels. Reversing your knife to the dull edge, press out the milk from the cobs. Add both to the soup along with the cooked beans. Heat through, taste once more for salt, and serve with minced fresh parsley.

Cream of Barley Soup
with whole barley, leeks, and mushrooms

I turned to a recipe from Najmieh Batmanglij, an Iranian food authority, for the notion of a creamy barley soup. I liked the idea of releasing barley from its eternal pairing with mushrooms, but when I took a sip of the finished soup, "mushrooms!" leapt immediately to mind. I swear I could taste them. Maybe mushrooms and barley are a tighter couple than I had thought. Because they do share an affinity, they appear here as a garnish, along with whole barley and leeks.

There are few ingredients in this simply made soup, but the long, slow browning of the onions gives it backbone. The barley, that trusty, chewy little grain, is used in two ways: half is cooked in the soup and then pureed with the broth and sour cream, making a luscious ivory-colored soup, the remainder added at the end, along with a julienned leek and sautéed mushrooms, to give the soup texture.

THE SOUP

$^1/_3$ cup barley
2 tablespoons olive oil
1 tablespoon butter
1 large or 2 medium onions, diced
$^1/_2$ teaspoon dried oregano or a big oregano sprig, if available
1 large leek (about $^1/_4$ pound), white part only, diced and rinsed
1 large carrot, grated
1 large garlic clove, chopped
Sea salt and freshly ground pepper
1 cup sour cream, can be reduced-fat

TO FINISH

$^1/_3$ cup barley
1 leek, white part only, halved, then slivered lengthwise into pieces about
    3 inches long
2 tablespoons butter
6 shiitake or other favorite mushrooms, thinly sliced

1. Cover the soup barley with hot water and set it aside while you prepare the rest of the ingredients.

For this soup, turn to a Chardonnay to complement the creaminess of the soup or a Pinot Noir if you prefer a red, which will pair well with the mushrooms.

2. Heat the oil and 1 tablespoon butter in a soup pot over medium heat until foaming. Add the onion and oregano, give a stir, and cook for 5 minutes. Then add the leek, carrot, and garlic. Cook for 10 minutes more, by which time a glaze will have formed on the bottom of the pan. Season with 1½ teaspoons salt.

3. Drain the barley and add it to the pot along with 6 cups water. Cook until the barley is soft, about 30 minutes, then puree the soup with the sour cream until smooth. Return the soup to the pot, taste for salt, and season with pepper. If it's too thick for your taste, add extra water or stock.

4. Rinse the remaining ⅓ cup barley, put it in a saucepan, and cover generously with water. Add a little salt and simmer until tender, about 30 minutes. Drain and keep warm. Simmer the leek in salted water until tender, after 5 minutes or so, drain, and toss in a little butter. Melt the remaining butter in a small skillet, add the mushrooms and a pinch of salt, and sauté over medium-high heat until golden, about 5 minutes. If the pan looks really dry, as it can with shiitake mushrooms, add ½ cup water and cook until the liquid is absorbed and the mushrooms have browned.

5. Serve the soup with a spoonful or two of the cooked barley in each bowl, the leeks and mushrooms piled on top, and a final twist of the peppermill.

Rice and Golden Turnip Soup
with fontina cheese

I love this soup. It's comfort food for those of us who love turnips. It's simple to make yet complex enough to be interesting. I've given this version a bit more glamour than its thin Italian predecessor by adding turnip's favorite herb, thyme, a pinch of nutmeg, and small bits of rich Fontina cheese.

Golden turnips have buttery yellow flesh that doesn't look like much until you put it against the white of the rice; then you can see how lovely it looks. In lieu of such a find, use your regular white turnip—tender new turnips in spring and summer and storage turnips in winter, thickly peeled.

3 tablespoons butter
1 onion, finely diced
1 large leek, white part only, diced (1 to 1½ cups) and rinsed
2 to 3 turnips (about ¾ pound), peeled and cut into ½-inch dice (about 2 cups)
Sea salt and freshly ground white pepper
2 garlic cloves, minced
Chunk of Parmigiano-Reggiano cheese rind
1 bushy thyme sprig or ½ teaspoon dried
¾ cup Arborio or other short-grain rice appropriate for risotto
6 cups simmering water or White Bean Broth (page 36)
Pinch of freshly grated nutmeg
½ cup small cubes of Italian Fontina cheese
1 tablespoon minced parsley
Freshly grated Parmigiano-Reggiano

It takes fifteen minutes to cook this soup and less to prepare the ingredients, but plan to serve it shortly after it's done, or the rice will continue to absorb the broth and you'll end up with a quasi-risotto rather than a soup. There are worse fates, though.

1. Melt the butter in a wide soup pot, then add the onion, leek, and turnips. Season with 1 teaspoon salt and give the mixture a stir. Add the garlic, cheese rind, and thyme, cover the pot, and cook over medium heat for 4 or 5 minutes.

Staying in the same region as Fontina, you might choose a Dolcetto to drink.

2. Add the rice to the pot and pour in the hot water. Bring to a boil, then lower the heat and simmer, covered, for 15 minutes. Remove the lid and add the nutmeg. Taste for salt and season with a little white pepper.

3. Distribute the Fontina among the soup bowls, ladle in the soup, and add a pinch of parsley and a lavish grating of Parmesan.

Quinoa, Corn, and Spinach Chowder

I absolutely adore this soup. It's a meal in a bowl that's just filling enough, plus you can have it on the table in less than thirty minutes. The liquid that comes from cooking the quinoa is so tasty that it becomes the chowder's broth.

The only caveat about quinoa is that it's important to rinse it very thoroughly in plenty of water before cooking to rid it of any traces of the slightly bitter saponin that naturally coats the grain. Mostly this has been done for you, but a good rinse is extra insurance. Otherwise, quinoa is perfect: a light, highly nutritious, quick-cooking grain. And this chowder is perfect for summer—or any time of the year.

$\frac{3}{4}$ cup quinoa, rinsed thoroughly under running water

2 ears corn, shucked

2 tablespoons olive oil

1 garlic clove, finely chopped

1 jalapeño chile, seeded and finely diced

Scant $\frac{1}{2}$ teaspoon ground cumin

Sea salt and freshly ground pepper

2 potatoes (about 6 ounces in all), peeled and cut into $\frac{1}{4}$-inch dice

$\frac{1}{4}$ pound feta cheese, cut into small cubes

1 bunch of spinach, stems removed and leaves washed

3 scallions, including a few of the greens, thinly sliced

$\frac{1}{3}$ cup chopped cilantro leaves

1 hard-cooked egg, peeled and diced, optional

A Greek white wine, such as a Moschofilero, might be just the match for this Peruvian-inspired soup, in spite of the distance between these countries. Closer to its original home, a Chilean Sauvignon Blanc could be poured as well.

1. Simmer the quinoa in 7 cups boiling water for 10 minutes. While the quinoa is cooking, slice off the top half of the corn kernels, then reverse your knife and press out the milk with the dull edge running down the length of the cobs. Drain the quinoa, but reserve the liquid.

2. Heat the oil in a 3-quart saucepan with the garlic and chile, cook for about 30 seconds over medium heat, then add the cumin, $\frac{1}{2}$ teaspoon salt, and the potatoes. Measure 6 cups of the quinoa-cooking water and add it to the pot. Bring to a boil,

then add the quinoa and simmer, partially covered, until the potatoes are tender, about 15 minutes. Add the corn and its scrapings.

3. Turn off the heat, taste for salt, and season the soup with pepper. Add the cheese, then stir in the spinach and the scallions. As soon as the spinach is wilted, after 2 to 3 minutes, serve the soup, garnished with the cilantro and the hard-cooked egg if you're using it.

Farro and Chickpea Soup
for winter

MAKES ABOUT
7 CUPS

This soup is almost monastic in character with its whole grains of farro (page 112) and chickpeas seasoned only with olive oil and rosemary. But perhaps it's because of its austerity that it manages to be such a satisfying soup.

While my preference is to cook the chickpeas from scratch, loading up the cooking water with garlic, sage, parsley, and such so that in the end it serves as a stock, this version uses organic canned chickpeas, an optional stock or Herb and Garlic Broth, plus a chunk of Parmigiano-Reggiano rind for flavor. The farro requires a soak but only twenty to thirty minutes to cook.

1½ cups farro, soaked for an hour or longer in cold water
2 to 4 tablespoons olive oil
1 onion, finely chopped
1 celery rib, finely diced
2 tablespoons *each* finely chopped rosemary and parsley
3 bay leaves
1 plump garlic clove, peeled
Chunk of Parmigiano-Reggiano cheese rind
6 cups Herb and Garlic Broth (page 43), Vegetable Stock (page 13), water, or stock
    plus water

One 15-ounce can chickpeas, preferably organic
Sea salt and freshly ground pepper

TO FINISH Extra virgin olive oil
1 teaspoon minced rosemary
Freshly grated Parmigiano-Reggiano

An appropriate match for this rustic soup would be a Chianti Classico or a Barbera. The wine needn't be the most expensive one available. A Chianti normale, rather than the riserva, will be fine.

1. Drain the farro. Heat the oil in a wide soup pot and add the onion, celery, rosemary, parsley, and bay leaves. Cook over medium heat, stirring occasionally, until the onion has softened but not browned, about 5 minutes. Add the garlic, cheese rind, drained farro, and broth. Bring to a boil, then cover the pan and simmer until the farro is tender, about 20 minutes.

2. If using organic canned chickpeas, strain the liquid into the soup. Cover the chickpeas with cool water, gently rub them together to loosen the skins, and discard them as they float to the surface. Then add the skinned chickpeas to the soup. They taste better and look nicer this way.

3. Taste for salt and season with pepper. Ladle the soup into bowls, drizzle over some olive oil, add the rosemary, and grate in a little cheese.

Farro and Spelt Farro is an ancient ancestor of wheat, as is spelt, and the two grains are often mentioned in the same breath—for good reason. Both have a pleasant nutty taste and good nutritional profiles and can be tolerated by those who can't tolerate the gluten in wheat. But they're not quite interchangeable. Farro, in my experience, cooks more quickly than spelt, and while soaking benefits the speed with which both grains cook, I find that a one-hour soak will be sufficient for farro, whereas spelt needs an overnight soak. Spelt grains tend to stay more separate and firm than farro, which yields more to the body of the dish it's found in. It can even be used to make a risotto-type dish called *farroto*. Spelt can be found at natural food stores. Farro, a bit more difficult to source, can be found at gourmet stores or online at www.ingredientsgourmet.com or www.cybercucina.com.

Farro and Chickpea Soup
for summer

Farro (page 112) and chickpeas needn't be relegated to the cold months—they make a fine summer soup too, when summer evenings are cool. Once the farro is soaked, this soup takes about fifteen minutes to put together and thirty minutes to cook.

1 cup farro, soaked in cold water for 1 hour, preferably longer
2 to 4 tablespoons olive oil
1 large onion, finely diced
1 celery rib, peeled if stringy, then finely diced
2 garlic cloves, chopped with a handful of parsley leaves
1 teaspoon tomato paste
1 cup finely diced or crushed fresh or canned tomatoes, with their juices
Sea salt and freshly ground pepper
One 15-ounce can chickpeas, preferably organic

TO FINISH   Small handful of basil leaves, finely slivered
Extra virgin olive oil
Freshly grated Parmigiano-Reggiano

We suggest an Italian white, such as a Soave from the Veneto, for this summer grain-based soup.

1. Drain the farro. Warm the olive oil in a wide soup pot. Add the onion, celery, and garlic-parsley mixture. Cook, stirring every so often, over medium heat until the onion is translucent and starting to soften, about 7 minutes. Stir in the tomato paste, then add the tomatoes, farro, 1 teaspoon salt, and 6 cups water.

2. Simmer for 30 minutes, covered, until the farro is tender but still toothsome. Remove the skins from the chickpeas (see page 112), then add them and, if organic, their liquid to the soup. (At this point the soup can sit at room temperature for several hours, giving the flavors a chance to meld.) Reheat if desired.

3. Ladle into bowls, season with pepper, stir in the basil and a few drops of olive oil, and grate a little Parmesan over the top.

Wild Rice Chowder

The combination of celery, celery root, and wild rice is such a beneficent one that I keep returning to it, even though mushrooms are also considered an excellent partner for this grain. Mushroom stock, in fact, makes a good cooking medium for wild rice. But this pretty vegetable chowder derives its stock from the rice-cooking water itself, much like the quinoa chowder on page 110. Its flavor is clean, the color golden-green, "like the water it grows in," a friend from Minnesota observed when we were cooking hand-harvested wild rice together.

This authentic wild rice (page 117) is quite different from—and superior to—the hybridized versions most of us are familiar with. Not that they aren't tasty, but you might want to try the real thing. The grains are gray and brown rather than jet black, and very delicious, some with a subtle parched taste. Traditional hand-gathered wild rice has been chosen by Slow Food USA as one of our valued but endangered American foods. To learn more, go to slowfoodusa.org and click on the Ark.

THE RICE

¾ cup wild rice, preferably traditional hand-harvested rice
½ teaspoon sea salt

THE SOUP VEGETABLES
(4 TO 5 CUPS IN ALL)

1 small onion, sliced
1 large or 2 smaller leeks, white parts only, sliced in rounds, separated, and rinsed well
1 or 2 carrots, sliced diagonally a scant ½ inch thick
1 small russet potato, peeled and cut into cubes
1 small celery root, peeled and diced
2 celery ribs, peeled if stringy and cut into long diagonals
1 fennel bulb, stalks discarded, a few fronds reserved, the bulb sliced lengthwise about ½ inch thick
2 tablespoons butter
Sea salt and freshly ground pepper
2 tablespoons flour

TO FINISH

½ cup cream or milk
A few tablespoons minced celery and/or fennel leaves

1. Rinse the rice, then add it to a pot with 6 cups water and ½ teaspoon salt. Bring to a boil, then lower the heat and simmer, covered, until the grains have started to burst and are pleasantly chewy, about 30 minutes. Pour the liquid off and set it aside to use in the soup. Re-cover the pot and set the rice aside to steam.

2. Peel, trim, and cut the vegetables, making the pieces attractive and on the large size, but not too big for a soupspoon.

3. Melt the butter in a wide soup pot, add the vegetables, and give them a stir. Cook over medium heat for several minutes, then add ½ teaspoon salt and the flour. Pour in the reserved rice-cooking liquid plus water to make 7 cups. Simmer until all the vegetables are tender, about 20 minutes. If you want the soup to be a little thicker, puree a cup or two of the vegetables and return them to the pot.

4. Add the rice and stir in the cream. Taste for salt and add more if needed. Season with pepper and serve with a generous sprinkling of minced celery or fennel leaves.

Choose an aromatic unoaked white, such as a Napa Valley Sauvignon Blanc, to drink with this chowder. Or, given the cream, you could also go with an oaked Sauvignon Blanc, such as that from Duckhorn or Spottswoode.

Native Wild Rice

Real wild rice, not the paddy-grown rice from California sold as "wild rice," is truly wild and hand-harvested. It grows in Minnesota, Michigan, Wisconsin, and parts of Canada and is still gathered in places by Native Americans. Unlike the shiny black grains of the cultivated varieties, the grains of true wild rice are gray and brownish, and they cook in far less time. Delicious parched rice can be purchased from the White Earth Land Recovery Project and is available through Native Harvest (www.nativeharvest.com or 1-888-779-3577). Real wild rice is also available at Zingerman's Deli in Ann Arbor, Michigan, and through www.heritagefoodsusa.com.

Spring vegetable soups are those that feature peas, asparagus, radishes, the first greens, the first turnips and fennel, wintered-over leeks, green onions, and chervil. All of these soups have the delicacy that spring vegetables and herbs provide, but they're not limited to a single expression. Simple variations can transform soups entirely, as demonstrated by the eight variations on a fresh pea soup or three variations on an asparagus soup. And it's the herbs—chervil, chives, the first lovage leaves (and even the first hothouse basil leaves)—that imbue these vegetable soups with the special flavor of spring.

While spring is not the bounteous season for soups, with or without the employment of herbs, there's nothing that says these soups can't be made at other times of year. Sorrel actually continues until the hard freeze, and where summers are coolish it thrives. Chard is a year-round garden vegetable for the most part; there is always a summer crop of leeks and maybe even a fall planting of peas. But if you're thinking and cooking locally and seasonally, these, for the most part, will be spring soups, whether your spring comes in February (those lucky Californians) or in May, for the rest of us.

Asparagus Soup
three ways

If you want to make
this earlier in the day
but still have that
bright green color,
pour the finished
soup immediately
into a bowl set over
ice, stir to cool it
down as quickly as
possible, then
refrigerate.

There's no reason to let your asparagus soup take on a dingy color and less than brilliant flavor. Just plan to serve within twenty minutes or so after making it, and it will have all the clarity one hopes to find in this vegetable.

Mercurial asparagus can go in many different directions, and here are three. The spring herbs such as chervil and chives (and their blossoms) are a natural; ginger crisped in brown butter is less usual but manages to be just as right, as does finishing the soup with a few drops of roasted sesame oil, black sesame seeds, and slivered cilantro. In all three, a few drops of lemon juice added just before serving bring all the elements smartly together.

1½ pounds asparagus, preferably thick spears
2 fat bunches of scallions, the greens set aside, the rest chopped (about 2 cups)
Bouquet garni: a few parsley sprigs, 1 bay leaf, a thyme sprig
Sea salt and freshly ground white pepper
2 tablespoons butter
Scant ¾ cup peeled and very thinly sliced potato
Few drops of fresh lemon juice, preferably from a Meyer lemon

*An herbaceous
Sauvignon Blanc from
the Napa Valley will be
good with all the
variations of this
spring soup.*

1. Snap off the ends of the asparagus where they break naturally and put them in a pot with 5 cups water, the scallion greens, and the bouquet garni. Add ½ teaspoon salt, bring to a boil, then simmer while you prepare everything else. If you're not ready to use the stock after 25 minutes, strain it and set aside.

2. Cut off the asparagus tips, cover them with cold water, and set aside to soak, agitating the water occasionally to get rid of any sand. Peel the remaining middles of the asparagus and chop them into ½-inch chunks.

3. Melt the butter in a soup pot. Add the scallions, asparagus middles, and potato. Give a stir, add a teaspoon of salt, and cook over medium-high heat for several minutes, just until the butter begins to brown a bit. Pour the hot stock through a

strainer right into the pot if you haven't strained it already, then simmer for 8 minutes. Puree in small batches until smooth. Set the strainer over a clean pot, pour the soup into it, and agitate it with a rubber scraper, finally pushing any debris against the strainer. Taste for salt and add a few drops of lemon juice to bring up the flavors. Season with a little white pepper.

4. Simmer the asparagus tips in a little salted water until tender, 4 to 6 minutes, then drain. Add them to the soup just before serving.

- *With Spring Herbs:* Garnish with plucked chervil or tarragon leaves, snipped chives, and their blossoms. If chervil is abundant, add a handful to the broth. Lovage—just 2 single leaves—one cooked in the stock and the other slivered over the finished soup, is another way to go.
- *With Ginger:* Peel a knob of ginger about an inch long and thinly slice it into julienne pieces. You'll want about 2 tablespoons. Heat 2 tablespoons butter until browned, then add the ginger and cook until golden and just starting to crisp, 4 to 6 minutes. Add the cooked asparagus tips and toss them with the ginger and butter. Serve the soup with a cluster of ginger and asparagus in each bowl.
- *With Sesame Oil:* Drizzle a few drops of roasted sesame oil over each bowl of soup. Sprinkle with toasted black or white sesame seeds and garnish with a pinch of finely slivered cilantro leaves. (If you love the flavor of fresh coriander, consider cooking 2 tablespoons of the minced stems along with the soup vegetables.)

Three Ways to Finish Your Asparagus Soup

Carrot Soup
with olive oil and minced carrot tops

Carrots are another versatile vegetable that go with most any herb or spice—cumin, cilantro, mint, chile, ginger, chervil, dill, and mixtures such as harissa and chermoula. However, with the first carrots of the season, you might find as I do that nothing is better than a carrot soup with a drizzle of olive oil and the spicy tops, finely minced. The greens have a wonderful warm fragrance, not unlike lovage or parsley, to which they're related. Set aside a few delicate greens for a garnish and simmer the rest with aromatics to make a simple, quick stock.

Regardless of the season, you'll want to make this when carrots are exceptionally sweet.

THE STOCK

Carrot peels and tops from the soup ingredients (below), a few of the finer greens reserved
½ onion, thinly sliced
1 thyme sprig
4 parsley sprigs
1 bay leaf
½ teaspoon sea salt

THE SOUP

1 tablespoon olive oil, plus extra for serving
1 onion, thinly sliced
¾ pound flavorful carrots, thinly sliced (about 2 cups)
1 small garlic clove, sliced
1 bay leaf
1 tablespoon chopped parsley
1 teaspoon white rice
Few drops of apple cider vinegar
Sea salt and freshly ground pepper

TO FINISH

¾ cup cooked rice, optional
Extra virgin olive oil
1 tablespoon minced carrot tops, parsley, or lovage

1. Put 5 cups water in a pot with the stock ingredients. Bring to a boil, then simmer, covered, for about 30 minutes.

2. Heat the oil in a soup pot over medium heat. Add the onion, carrots, garlic, bay leaf, parsley, and rice. Cook for a few minutes, then add ½ cup water, cover the pot, and cook for 5 minutes more. Meanwhile, pour the stock through a strainer into a 1-quart measure. Add water if necessary to make a quart and add the stock to the pot. Simmer until the carrots are soft, 15 to 20 minutes.

3. Puree the soup, then return it to the pot. Add a few drops of vinegar, then taste for salt. Pour the soup over the rice if you're using it, drizzle olive oil over the top, sprinkle on the minced carrot tops, and season with pepper.

For wine, a crisp, medium-bodied Oregon Pinot Gris from the King Estate or Chehalem will stand up to the sweetness of the carrots.

Fennel and Almond Soup
with saffron and ricotta dumplings

MAKES 5 TO 6 CUPS

Try this pretty golden first-course soup when fennel and fresh peas are in season. It's thickened with finely ground almonds, which give it a creamy feel and a subtle nutty flavor. To make this even more special, I bake ricotta covered with fennel seeds, cut it into triangles, and add three pieces to each bowl. The heat wilts the triangles to dumpling tenderness, and you can make them well ahead of time.

Almonds ground in a little hand mill come out light and feathery and literally melt into the soup. Lacking that, use your food processor, although they will be a little grainier.

THE STOCK
2 cups chopped fennel stalks
Roots and 1 cup chopped paler leek greens
1 cup celery tips and leaves
1 bay leaf
Handful of parsley stems
Sea salt and freshly ground pepper

THE RICOTTA DUMPLINGS	1 pound ricotta cheese
	Olive oil
	1 tablespoon fennel or anise seeds

THE SOUP	1 large or 2 smaller fennel bulbs (about 1 pound), quartered and cored
	2 to 3 tablespoons butter or a combination of butter and olive oil
	2 leeks, white parts only (about $\frac{1}{4}$ pound), quartered, chopped, and rinsed
	1 celery rib, thinly sliced
	2 tablespoons chopped parsley
	$\frac{1}{2}$ cup almonds, blanched and finely ground
	2 pinches of saffron threads
	1 cup, more or less, shelled fresh or frozen peas
	Finely minced fennel greens for garnish

Viognier, an aromatic and complex wine, sometimes with a hint of almond, would be perfect with this soup, especially one from Napa Valley's Stags' Leap Winery.

1. Preheat the oven to 350°F.

2. Put the vegetable trimmings in a pot with 7 cups water, the bay leaf, the parsley, and $\frac{1}{2}$ teaspoon salt. Bring to a boil, reduce the heat, and simmer, covered, for about 25 minutes.

3. Press the ricotta into a 6-cup dish brushed with olive oil and sprinkle the fennel seeds over the top. Bake until golden and firm, about 30 minutes. Cut into triangles and set aside. You can make the soup while it's baking.

4. Slice the fennel into pieces that will fit in a soupspoon. Melt the butter in a soup pot and add the vegetables and parsley. Season with a teaspoon of salt, toss them around to coat, and cook over medium heat for about 5 minutes. Add the almonds and saffron and cook for several minutes. Strain the stock. You should have about 6 cups or a little less. Add the hot stock to the soup vegetables, bring it to a boil, then lower the heat and simmer for 20 minutes, or until the vegetables are soft but not mushy. Add the peas during the last 3 or 4 minutes. Taste for salt and season with pepper.

5. Serve the soup in soup plates or small bowls. Add 3 pieces of the baked ricotta to each bowl, sprinkle with the minced fennel greens, and serve.

Leek and Scallion Soup
with potato gnocchi

A variation on a classic, here the potatoes are found mostly in the gnocchi and the leeks in the soup, which can be pureed or not, as you like. A soup for all seasons, it's particularly good in the spring, when brand-new scallions, or spring onions, first make their appearance. This soup also provides a good place to dispense with some truffle oil. A few drops in each bowl makes it a soup to begin a special meal.

THE SOUP

2 tablespoons butter
4 cups chopped and rinsed leeks, white parts only (5 to 6 medium leeks)
1 celery rib, peeled and chopped
1 small russet potato (4 to 6 ounces), peeled and diced
Sea salt and freshly ground pepper
½ cup dry white wine

TO FINISH

Frozen potato gnocchi
1 tablespoon butter
1 cup finely slivered scallion, including an inch or 2 of the greens

1. Melt the butter in a soup pot, then add the leeks, celery, and potato. Season with a teaspoon of salt and cook over medium heat, stirring occasionally, until the leeks have softened, about 10 minutes. Add the wine and allow it to cook mostly away, after about 3 minutes, then add 1 quart water. Bring to a boil, lower the heat, and simmer, covered, until the potatoes have softened, about 20 minutes. Cool briefly, then puree a cup of the soup and return it to the pot. (Or puree all of the soup quickly so that the potato doesn't turn gummy.) Season with pepper.

2. Simmer the gnocchi in salted water until they rise to the surface and are tender, 4 or 5 minutes. Scoop them onto a plate, cover, and set aside in a warm place. Melt the butter in a small skillet, add the scallions, and cook just to wilt them.

3. Serve the soup, swirl in the scallions, and add a few gnocchi to each.

A crisp white, an Arneis or a Tuscan Vernaccia, would go well with the leeks and scallions.

vegetable soups for spring

Pea Soup
eight ways

Spring would not be spring without at least one soup made of fresh pod peas, but here are eight variations to tempt you. A fresh pea soup should be substantially different from one made of dried peas, which means it should be cooked briefly and served instantly. Since it takes but a few minutes to make the soup, spend an extra twenty minutes to make a stock as long as you have fresh peas.

THE STOCK

I teaspoon butter *· olive oil*
I bunch of scallions, including the greens, chopped *- chives*
6 large parsley branches *· mint*
8 butter lettuce leaves (outer leaves are fine), torn
Sea salt and freshly ground white pepper
3 cups clean pea pods

THE SOUP

I teaspoon unsalted butter *· olive oil*
½ cup thinly sliced scallion, spring onion, or young leek, white parts only
2 pounds fresh peas with bright green moist-looking pods, or 2 cups frozen peas
½ teaspoon sugar *· pinch*

Accompany this spring soup with a cool-climate Sauvignon Blanc from New Zealand, keeping in step with the cool-climate peas.

1. To make the stock, melt the butter in a 2-quart pot. Add the scallions, parsley, lettuce, and ½ teaspoon salt. Cook over medium heat until wilted, about 3 minutes. Pour in 5 cups water, add the pea pods, and bring to a boil. Lower the heat and simmer, covered, for 20 minutes, then strain.

2. For the soup, melt the butter in a soup pot and add the sliced scallion. Cook over medium heat for about a minute, then add ½ cup of the stock (or water if you're using frozen peas) so that the scallion stews without browning. After 4 to 5 minutes, add the peas, ½ teaspoon salt, and the sugar. Pour in 2½ cups of the stock (or water), bring to a boil, and simmer for 3 minutes.

3. Transfer the soup to a blender. Drape a towel over the lid and give it a few short pulses to make sure it won't splatter, then puree at high speed for I minute. Taste

for salt and season with pepper. Pour into small soup bowls and serve immediately with any of the garnishes and additions suggested below.

- *Spring Pea Soup with Chervil and Chives:* A delicate spring herb, chervil is complex, tender, and interesting with its licorice overtones. Chives are usually in bloom when peas are in season. Mince a handful of chervil and stir it into the soup just before serving. Finely slice or snip a few chives. Separate a clump of blossoms at the base. Garnish each bowl with a delicate sprig of chervil, a shower of chives, and a few chive blossoms.
- *Spring Pea Soup with Cream:* Stir a spoonful or two of thick organic cream into the soup and garnish with chervil or the first leaves of basil, finely slivered. Add small crisp croutons if you wish.
- *Spring Pea Soup with Truffle Oil:* Drizzle a few drops of truffle oil into each bowl.
- *Spring Pea Soup with Basil Puree:* Blanch several basil leaves, rinse them in cold water, then puree with a few teaspoons olive oil and a pinch of salt. Stir the puree into the soup.
- *Spring Pea Soup with Green Garlic:* Slice a small head of green garlic and stew it with the onions when you make the soup. The greens can go into the stock. While delicate, the garlic will be a dominant flavor, so don't expect a pure pea taste.
- *Spring Pea Soup with Slivered Peas:* Sliver, on the diagonal, a few very tender snow peas or edible-pod peas. Pour boiling water over them, then use them to garnish the soup. Include a cluster of pea shoots in each bowl.
- *Chilled Spring Pea Soup:* Have a bowl full of ice and water ready. Puree the soup, pour it into a second bowl, and set it over the ice. Stir to bring down the temperature quickly. This will preserve its color and fresh pea taste.
- *Spring Pea Soup with Herb and Blossom Butter:* Mix 4 tablespoons soft butter with 1½ tablespoons finely chopped herbs, drawing from chives, chervil, parsley, lemon thyme, basil, and 2 tablespoons slivered or chopped blossoms, such as sage, rosemary, borage, calendula, and nasturtiums. Season with a pinch of salt. Add a teaspoon to each bowl and let it melt, releasing its fragrance and flavor. Roll the leftover butter into a log and freeze for another use.

Spring Vegetable Medley
of turnips, radishes, asparagus, and peas

This little vegetable soup celebrates the market not only in spring but again in the fall. I have made this soup from my farmers' market produce both in early June and in September—minus the asparagus. The high-altitude coolness of northern New Mexico is kind to turnips, peas, and sorrel. Leek trimmings, asparagus stems, and pea pods are great stock ingredients, so you might as well make a little stock while you cut your vegetables.

This light, clean soup is best served as soon as it has finished cooking while everything about it is fresh and new. You can enrich it by adding a pea-size lump of butter or a spoonful of crème fraîche to each serving or simply leave it as it is. I sometimes cook a handful of dried Italian tortellini and add three or four to each bowl, which makes it more filling.

Handful of snow peas or edible-pod peas
Stock vegetables: 1 celery rib, 1 large carrot, 1 garlic clove, handful of parsley,
     handful of leek greens, asparagus stalks, all chopped, optional
Sea salt
9 or 10 small fresh turnips (about ¾ pound or 2 cups)
12 radishes
1 tablespoon butter
1 bay leaf
2 bushy thyme sprigs or ¼ teaspoon dried
1 cup leeks, sliced in ¼-inch rounds and rinsed (about 4 small leeks)
4 green garlic cloves, thinly sliced
8 asparagus spears, peeled and the top 3 inches sliced off
½ pound fresh peas, shelled, or ½ cup frozen
1 tablespoon minced parsley
1 tablespoon chopped tarragon or chervil

1. If you want to make a stock, bring 5 cups water to a boil. Add the pea pods to the water as it's heating along with the other stock vegetables. Add a few pinches of salt, bring to a boil, then simmer while you peel and cut the vegetables for the

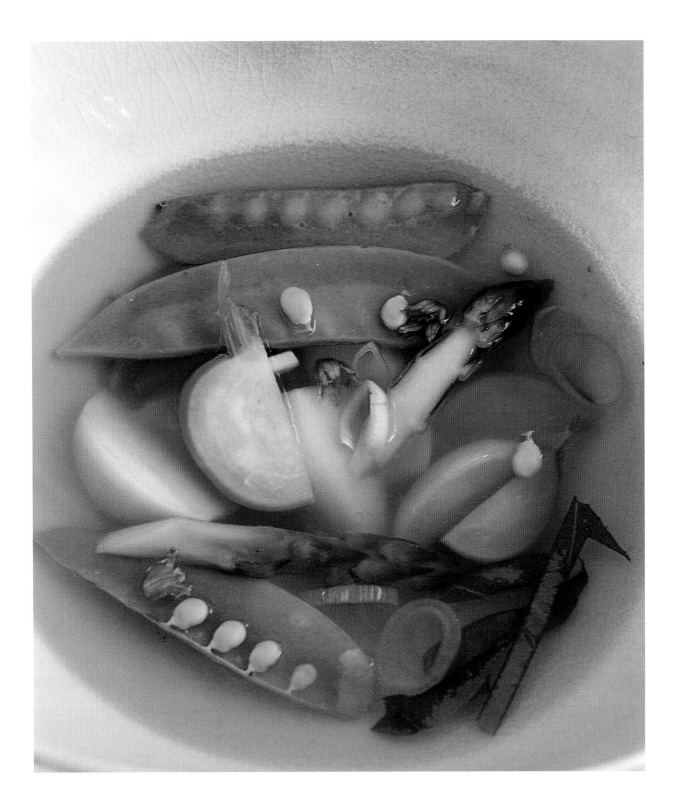

soup. Neatly peel the turnips with 5 or 6 even strokes of a paring knife. Halve them and cut each half into thirds. Cut the radishes into halves or quarters, depending on their size.

Although wine may be difficult to pair with the vegetables in this dish, sparkling wines are versatile enough that they might make a good match. Try the Scharffenberger from Anderson Valley in Mendocino.

2. Melt the butter in a soup pot over medium-low heat with the bay leaf and thyme. Add the leek and garlic, cook for 2 or 3 minutes, then add the turnips and radishes. Season with ¾ teaspoon salt. Cover and cook over low heat for 4 minutes while you strain the stock. You should have about 1 quart.

3. Add the stock to the turnips, bring to a boil, then simmer, covered, until the turnips are tender, about 15 minutes. Add the asparagus during the last 5 minutes, the peas during the last minute. Divide the broth and vegetables among four bowls and sprinkle over the parsley and tarragon.

MAKES 6 CUPS

Green Spring Soup
of spinach, lettuce, and sorrel

Most soups become gorgeous as their ingredients take on heat, but this one is on the homely side—the sorrel turns an army green, and lettuce goes blah in moments. The vibrancy of this soup lies in its bright flavors, which are robust and stimulating, and its looks improve once it's pureed and garnished.

Good chilled and hot.

2 tablespoons butter, plus extra butter for the croutons
1 large leek, white part only, chopped (scant 2 cups)
2 small potatoes, peeled, quartered, and thinly sliced (1 scant cup)
1 garlic clove, slivered
1 bunch of spinach, stems removed and leaves washed and chopped, or 2 cups
   chard or beet greens
1 to 2 cups sorrel, slivered

4 cups chopped lettuce

2 tablespoons *each* chopped parsley, tarragon, and basil

Sea salt and freshly ground pepper

6 cups water, Vegetable Stock (page 13), or chicken stock

Fresh lemon juice to taste

TO FINISH   1 cup small bread cubes without crusts

2 tablespoons butter

¼ cup cream

A spicy red, like a Côtes-du-Rhône, stands up to the earthiness of these greens.

1. Melt the butter in a wide soup pot over medium heat, then add the leek, potatoes, and garlic. Cook for several minutes, then add the greens and herbs and season with 1 teaspoon salt. Give them a stir, add the liquid, and bring to a boil. Simmer, partially covered, until the potatoes are tender, about 20 minutes.

2. Puree the soup. Taste it for salt, season with pepper, then add a few drops of lemon juice to sharpen the flavors.

3. Crisp the bread cubes in the butter over medium-low heat until golden, 6 to 8 minutes. Serve the soup with the cream stirred in just at the end, leaving nice fat streaks, and the croutons.

Five Variations

- Include a handful of celery leaves and/or a celery rib, chopped.
- Include a lovage leaf or a stalk of Chinese celery in the soup and add a slivered leaf of either at the very end. Both perk up a soup greatly.
- Thicken the soup with a slice of bread or a little cooked rice rather than potato.
- Include other greens, such as watercress, borage, or wild nettles.
- Garnish with sunflower sprouts or herb blossoms: chive, golden mustard, calendula or nasturtium, or anise hyssop.

A Green Tortilla Soup

MAKES ABOUT
2 QUARTS

I have eaten tortilla soups of all kinds, from chicken broth with tortilla strips to cream-based Mexican "hotel" versions, from spicy red broths to thick tomato purees served with those scary red-dyed tortilla chips, and so on. This version, which is based on a chard and cilantro stock, is green and lively tasting. You can either serve it as a broth, crowned with a cluster of yellow strips of corn tortillas, or puree the soup and then add the garnishes. This amount will serve four for a meal, six for appetizers; if one batch is too much for your household, serve it brothy the first night and pureed the second.

Tortilla soup usually depends on a rich chicken stock, so making a good vegetable stock at the very least is advised. It does much to enhance the soup.

While the stock is simmering, you can ready the soup vegetables and fry the tortilla strips. The soup itself takes about twenty minutes.

THE SOUP AND STOCK

3 tablespoons light olive or sunflower seed oil

4 large garlic cloves, unpeeled

2 white onions, 1 roughly chopped, the other finely chopped

2 large Roma or plum tomatoes, halved

1 cup coarsely chopped cilantro stems plus 1 cup finely chopped leaves

1 hefty bunch of chard, stems coarsely chopped, leaves finely chopped and set aside

1 cup coarsely chopped celery plus 1 cup finely diced celery

2 carrots, sliced

1 bay leaf

2 corn tortillas

Sea salt

1 good-sized bunch of scallions, including the firm greens, finely sliced

1 tablespoon finely diced jalapeño chile

TO FINISH

¾ cup peanut oil for frying

4 corn tortillas, quartered and cut into narrow strips

Small cubes of Monterey Jack cheese, about 1 tablespoon per serving

1 large lime, cut into quarters or sixths

1. Heat half the oil in a soup pot and add the unpeeled garlic cloves and roughly chopped onion. Cook over medium-low heat, turning occasionally. The aim is to

soften the garlic within its skin and lightly brown the onion. It should take about 10 minutes.

Mexican beer would be better here than wine.

2. Next add the tomatoes, cilantro stems, chard stems, coarsely chopped celery, carrots, and bay leaf. Tear the tortillas into quarters and add them to the pot. Add 2 quarts water and 1 teaspoon salt. Bring to a boil, then lower the heat and simmer, uncovered, for 25 minutes. Pour the stock through a strainer.

3. Rinse the chard leaves, then chop into squares that will fit comfortably in a soupspoon. Heat the ¾ cup peanut oil in a small frying pan and, when hot enough to sizzle a single tortilla strip, add the strips, in 2 batches if the pan is crowded. Fry until golden and crisp. Transfer the strips to paper towels and set aside. Or lay the tortilla strips on a sheet pan and bake them in a 400°F oven until crisp.

4. To complete the soup, heat the remaining 1½ tablespoons olive oil in a wide soup pot over medium heat. Add the finely chopped onion and cook for several minutes, stirring occasionally, then add the scallions, finely diced celery, cilantro leaves, jalapeño, and chard leaves. Season with 1 teaspoon salt, cook for several minutes, until the chard begins to lose its volume, then pour in the strained stock. Simmer for 15 minutes. Taste for salt, but remember that the lime will sharpen the soup, too.

5. Ladle the soup into bowls. Add the cheese and perch a cluster of tortilla strips on top. Serve a lime wedge with each bowl.

Summer soups are ideal for appetites that have been dampened by the heat, and chilled summer soups make a refreshing contrast to the sweltering humidity that permeates so much of our country. A lot of soups that are usually served hot are also good tepid or chilled—the Farro and Chickpea Soup for Summer on page 114, for example, any roasted vegetable soup, beet soups, or the carrot soup with carrot tops on page 122. Add a spritz of fresh lemon juice or a splash of vinegar to soups that are normally eaten hot, and suddenly they're just as appealing cold. On the other hand, you might find that a hot soup on a summer's day has a rather cooling effect, even if you're not craving warmth. They manage to make you feel cool.

Of course what makes the idea of summer soups especially compelling is all the produce that's available for soup making—tomatoes, corn, squash, peppers. Some of this carries into fall too, as you'll discover in the next chapter.

Avocado Soup
with herbs, slivered radishes, and pistachios

Avocado pureed with buttermilk (low-fat) and yogurt (with the cream on top) yields a pale green soup laced with masses of minced herbs, textured with cucumber, and garnished with slivered radishes, herbs, and green pistachios. All in all, it's a fine soup for a hot day, and although the recipe makes just a scant quart, it will be enough for four or more servings.

2 cups low-fat buttermilk

1 cup yogurt, preferably whole-milk

1 large avocado, peeled and pitted

1 cucumber, peeled and seeded

1 large garlic clove

Sea salt and freshly ground pepper

3 slender scallions, white parts plus a bit of the green, finely minced

2 tablespoons chopped dill

1 tablespoon snipped chives

1 tablespoon minced marjoram or oregano

1 tablespoon minced tarragon

1 tablespoon chopped cilantro

½ jalapeño chile, seeded and chopped

Zest and juice of 1 lime

½ teaspoon sweetener, such as agave syrup (page 140), to taste

TO FINISH

Finely sliced chives and chive blossoms

Thinly slivered radishes

Dill, mint, and cilantro sprigs

⅓ cup shelled pistachios or walnuts

1. Puree the buttermilk, yogurt, avocado, and a quarter of the peeled cucumber in a blender until smooth, then pour it into a bowl.

2. Mash the garlic with ½ teaspoon salt and stir it into the puree along with the scallions, herbs, chile, and lime zest. Season to taste with salt, pepper, lime juice, and sweetener, if needed. Seed and finely dice the remaining cucumber and add to the soup. Cover and refrigerate until well chilled. Just before serving, taste and correct the seasonings.

3. Ladle the soup into bowls, then cover the surface with the chives, radishes, herb sprigs, and pistachios.

Agave Syrup For those who don't like using refined sugar, organic or not, agave syrup offers an alternative. It's sweeter than sugar but has a low glycemic index. While there's more to it than pure sweetness, its flavor is not as pronounced as that of honey or maple syrup. Derived from agave, the same plant used for making tequila, the liquid form of the syrup is easy to add to foods as it dissolves instantly. Agave syrup can be found at natural food stores.

MAKES 3 TO 4 CUPS

Cool Cucumber Soup
with a cucumber-herb relish

This herb-green froth of a soup can be whipped together in a blender in moments, then chilled until serving. Served in glasses, it makes a refreshing way to begin a summer dinner, and it's a great convenience to have on hand in the refrigerator for a quick lunch or an afternoon bite.

A cucumber soup can be led in many directions. You can allow dill to predominate and garnish it with dill flowers, use a mixture of herbs as is done here, or use any one of them alone. I find a mixture most interesting—dill, basil, cilantro, and chives with a leaf or two of lovage, the perfect cucumber herb in my opinion. If you want the snap of chile, add minced jalapeño and lime.

2 pounds cucumbers

1 cup buttermilk, whole-milk yogurt, sour cream, or a mixture

½ cup coarsely chopped herbs, including basil, dill, cilantro, and lovage

Sea salt and freshly ground pepper

Zest and juice of 2 lemons, or to taste

THE CUCUMBER RELISH

2 tablespoons minced chives or scallions

1 tablespoon minced dill

2 tablespoons *each* finely chopped basil and cilantro

1 lovage leaf, finely slivered

2 teaspoons olive oil

You can make the soup ultra-lean if you use buttermilk or richer with sour cream. I fall in between, using buttermilk along with at least a cup of the best whole-milk yogurt I can find, such as Strauss Family Organic Creamery.

1. Peel and seed the cucumbers. Use one to make a cup of small dice and set it aside, then coarsely chop the rest. Puree in a blender or food processor with the buttermilk, chopped herbs, ½ teaspoon salt, and the zest and juice from 1 lemon. Chill.

2. Just before serving, toss the reserved diced cucumber with the herbs, a few pinches of salt, the olive oil, and the remaining lemon juice and zest.

3. Taste the soup for salt, pepper, and acidity, adding more lemon juice if needed, then serve in chilled bowls with the cucumber-herb relish.

Crookneck Squash Soup
with salsa verde

MAKES 2 QUARTS

You can't go wrong with the combination of squash, herbs, and, in this case, some pasta. And while you can use any kind of summer squash, this soup offers an especially nice way to feature the delicate crookneck. Should you have some squash blossoms, slice them thinly and add them at the end as a sunny garnish.

Given that water is the liquid, a generous quarter cup of fresh herbs—equal parts oregano, parsley, sage, and a sprig of thyme—is used to create a bit of a broth. A salsa verde, stirred in before serving, makes what is a very simple soup stellar.

THE SOUP

1 pound crookneck or other summer squash

2 teaspoons *each* butter and olive oil

1 onion, thinly sliced

¼ cup finely chopped herbs, including oregano or marjoram, parsley, sage, and a
sprig or 2 of thyme

Sea salt and freshly ground pepper

4½ cups water or vegetable stock featuring summer vegetables (page 10) or White
Bean Broth (page 36)

1 cup dried pasta, such as small shells, farfalle, or other small shapes

THE SALSA VERDE

1 shallot, finely diced

6 tablespoons finely chopped parsley, preferably flat-leaf

3 tablespoons finely chopped mixed herbs, such as tarragon, basil, marjoram, and dill

2 tablespoons capers, rinsed and chopped

Grated zest and juice of 1 small lemon, or to taste

1 small garlic clove, minced

½ cup extra virgin olive oil

For wine, go with a spicy Gewürztraminer from Navarro winery in California's Anderson Valley.

1. Slice the bulb end of the squash lengthwise into quarters, then again crosswise a scant ½ inch thick. Slice the necks into rounds ½ inch thick.

2. Warm the butter and oil in a soup pot over medium-high heat. Add the onion, squash, and herbs, give it a stir, and cook for 5 minutes. Season with ¾ teaspoon salt, then add the water or stock. Bring to a boil, then lower the heat and simmer, covered, until the squash is tender, about 15 minutes. Taste for salt and season with pepper.

3. Make the salsa verde: Put the shallot, herbs, capers, lemon zest, and garlic in a bowl with ⅜ teaspoon salt and a little pepper. Stir in the olive oil, then add lemon juice to taste.

4. Boil the pasta in salted water, then drain. Add the pasta to the finished soup and serve with a spoonful of salsa verde in each bowl.

White Corn Chowder
with a smoky swirl

I mention white corn not because I prefer it to yellow, but because it's become so popular that in many markets it seems to have replaced yellow corn entirely. White corn is sweet and delicious, which is why it's so popular, but it can make pale and anemic-looking soup. The very sweetness of today's corn varieties encourages us to turn away from sweet herbs, like basil and marjoram, even though they are a natural choice in summer, when corn is in season. Instead, I find the more grounding notes of thyme, parsley, and bay work best.

6 ears sweet corn, shucked (about 4 cups kernels)
Aromatics: 1 bay leaf, 1 thyme sprig, and 6 parsley stems for the stock, plus
    4 parsley branches, 1 bay leaf, and 1 large thyme sprig, tied together with
    string for the soup
1 celery rib, diced, a few leaves reserved
2 onions, finely diced, trimmings reserved
4 medium size yellow-fleshed or other summer potatoes, peeled and diced into
    $^{1}/_{2}$-inch cubes (about 1$^{1}/_{2}$ cups), peels reserved if organic
1 yellow bell pepper, peeled and cut into $^{1}/_{2}$-inch dice, core reserved
3 tablespoons butter
2 small garlic cloves
2 teaspoons Spanish smoked paprika (page 92)
1 tablespoon flour
1 cup milk plus 1 cup light or heavy cream, or 2 cups milk
Sea salt and freshly ground pepper
1 teaspoon *each* minced parsley, thyme, and snipped chives

1. Heat 6 cups water in a saucepan. While it's heating, slice the top half of the kernels from each ear of corn and put them in a bowl. Reversing your knife, press down on the cobs with the dull edge to extract the milk and set it aside in another bowl. As you finish, break the corncobs in half and add them to the water along with the aromatics for the stock, a few leaves from the celery rib, the onion trim-

To make a tasty corn chowder without bacon and chicken stock, I milk all the essence I can from the cobs in a quickly assembled stock. As for the traditional addition of heavy cream, if you want to forgo its calories, you can puree a cup of the vegetables with extra stock or milk, then stir it back into the pot.

For wine, stay with the
classic match of
Chardonnay with corn,
choosing a richer New
World Chardonnay,
such as one from Napa
Valley's Beringer
winery.

mings, the potato peels (if organic), and the pepper core. Bring to a boil, lower the heat, and simmer, covered, for 25 minutes.

2. Melt 2 tablespoons of the butter in a wide soup pot. Add the celery, onions, potatoes, bell pepper, garlic, and a teaspoon of the paprika. Stir to coat, then add ½ cup water. Add the herb bundle, then cover and cook over medium heat until the onions are soft, about 10 minutes. Stir in the flour and continue cooking while you strain the stock. Pour 1 quart of the stock into the pot, then add a cup of milk, the corn scrapings, and all but a cup of the corn kernels. Simmer, covered, for 15 minutes, add the remaining corn kernels, cook for a minute longer, then turn off the heat. Remove the herb bundle and add the cream if you're using it, or the second cup of milk. Taste for salt and season with pepper.

3. Melt the remaining tablespoon of butter in a small skillet until it foams and begins to brown a little. Stir in the remaining teaspoon of paprika and turn off the heat. Ladle the soup into bowls and add a few drops of the red butter to each, plus a sprinkling of the minced parsley, thyme, and chives.

MAKES 6 CUPS

Curried Coconut Corn Soup
with yogurt and lime

This is one of those soups that's good warm, tepid, and even chilled. Warm, it's quite pleasant poured over a mound of basmati rice, garnished with sprigs of cilantro and a wedge of lime. This soup can also be chunky or smooth. For a creamy-smooth soup, blend it at high speed for at least three minutes. Or puree just a cup to thicken the background and leave the rest full of texture.

4 ears corn, yellow or white varieties, shucked
8 cilantro branches plus 2 tablespoons finely chopped

½ cup finely diced red onion, trimmings reserved

1 tablespoon butter or roasted peanut oil (page 24)

½ teaspoon ground turmeric

1 teaspoon ground coriander

½ teaspoon ground cumin

½ teaspoon hot or mild paprika

½ teaspoon garam masala

Sea salt and freshly ground pepper

1 tablespoon flour

1 can light or regular coconut milk (1½ to 2 cups)

Juice of 1 lime, or more to taste

½ cup yogurt

Cilantro sprigs for garnish

1. Heat 6 cups water in a saucepan. Meanwhile, slice the corn off the cobs, taking just the top halves of the kernels, then reverse your knife and run the dull edge down the cobs to press out the liquid. Break the cobs and put them in the heating water with the cilantro branches and any onion trimmings. Simmer for at least 15 minutes—longer if you can—then strain.

An Alsatian Pinot Gris plays well with the spices in this soup.

2. Melt the butter in a soup pot over medium heat. Add the onion, cook for 3 to 4 minutes, then add all the spices and cook for a few minutes more. Stir in the flour, pour in the coconut milk, and add the corn and the scrapings, the chopped cilantro, 1½ cups stock, and 1 teaspoon salt. If the soup is too thick, thin it with more water. Simmer over medium heat for 10 minutes. Squeeze in the lime juice and taste, adjusting the salt if needed. Refrigerate if you want to serve the soup chilled.

3. Beat the yogurt with a fork until smooth. Serve the soup with a swirl of yogurt and sprigs of cilantro in each bowl.

Potato and Fennel Soup
with rouille

If you cut the pieces larger and use less liquid, you'll end up with more of a stew. For a soup, though, cut all the vegetables into chunks that will fit comfortably into a soupspoon.

This can be a real farmers' market soup for a July day when leeks, potatoes, garlic, fennel, and even tomatoes are to be had. I make a stock with the vegetable trimmings and some additional herbs. In fact even with this stock or the more elaborate Vegetable Stock (page 13) using summer vegetables, the soup will taste a little thin until you add the rouille. Then everything will come together nicely.

Serve with a plate of grilled rustic bread rubbed with a clove of garlic and brushed generously with olive oil. For wine, chilled Provençal whites or rosés would be just right with this soup.

1 large leek

2 medium fennel bulbs (about 10 ounces)

4 parsley sprigs

$\frac{1}{2}$ onion, cut into chunks

1 carrot, cut into chunks

Aromatics: 2 pinches of saffron threads, $\frac{1}{2}$ teaspoon fennel seed, 2 thyme sprigs, 3 bay leaves

Sea salt and freshly ground pepper

3 tablespoons olive oil, plus a little for the stock

8 small red or yellow summer potatoes (about $1\frac{1}{4}$ pounds)

1 garlic clove, minced

2 teaspoons tomato paste

$\frac{1}{2}$ cup dry white wine

5 fresh or canned Roma or plum tomatoes, peeled, seeded, and chopped, juices strained and reserved

THE ROUILLE

1 slice firm white bread, crusts removed

3 garlic cloves, peeled

$\frac{1}{2}$ teaspoon sea salt

2 teaspoons ground red chile, such as New Mexican chile (not chili powder)

$\frac{1}{4}$ cup extra virgin olive oil

1. To make the stock, heat 2 quarts water in a pot. Meanwhile, cut off the leek roots and chop 1 cup of the tender greens. Trim the fennel bulb and cut off the stalks. Add the leek roots and greens, a good handful of the fennel greens and stalks, the parsley, onion, and carrot to the water along with one of the thyme sprigs and one of the bay leaves, 1 scant teaspoon salt, and a splash of olive oil. Bring to a boil, then lower the heat and simmer, uncovered, while you assemble everything else and start the soup.

2. Peel the potatoes with a paring knife (add the peels to the stock), halve them, then cut them into $\frac{1}{2}$-inch pieces. Chop the fennel bulb into irregular $\frac{1}{2}$-inch pieces, reserving some of the remaining greens for garnish. Quarter the leek lengthwise, slice into small pieces, and rinse well.

3. Warm the 3 tablespoons oil in a heavy pot and add the potatoes, fennel bulb, leek, garlic, and remaining aromatics. Cook over medium heat for several minutes, or until things start sticking, then add $\frac{1}{2}$ cup water. Cover and cook for 10 minutes, then stir in the tomato paste and cook for a minute. Add the wine and cook until it has simmered away to syrup, after 3 minutes or so, then add the tomatoes, $\frac{1}{2}$ teaspoon salt, and a few twists of pepper plus the reserved tomato juice and enough strained stock to make 7 cups. Simmer, covered, for 25 minutes. Let cool a little, then taste for salt and season with pepper.

4. To make the rouille, moisten the bread with a few tablespoons water. Smash the garlic in a mortar with the salt to make a paste, then squeeze the bread of excess moisture and add it to the mortar along with the chile. Continue pounding until smooth. While stirring, gradually add the oil until all is amalgamated into a thick red sauce. Serve a spoonful in each bowl and garnish with the reserved fennel greens, finely chopped.

✓Scallion and New Potato Soup
with a tomato salad

Forget those so-called red new potatoes from the grocery store. Real new potatoes aren't a variety but simply any newly dug potato. As summer is their season, it stands to reason that August is just as good a time for potato soups as February, but with a lighter touch employed. Made with scallions, this quickly assembled soup has a pale green hue and is finished with a little salad of chopped tomatoes and slivered basil. Orange Sun Golds, yellow pear, and green zebra make a particularly striking garnish. The soup can be served hot or tepid.

THE SOUP

2 big bunches of green onions (scallions or table onions), including the firm
    greens
1 pound new potatoes, any variety or a mixture of varieties, scrubbed
1 tablespoon *each* butter and olive oil
Sea salt and freshly ground pepper

THE TOMATO SALAD

¾ to 1 cup halved or diced fresh tomatoes, such as small cherry or pear types
Several opal or Italian basil leaves, finely slivered
1 shallot, finely diced
1 tablespoon extra virgin olive oil

For wine, serve a lightly chilled Italian red, such as a Valpolicella.

1. Slice the scallions about ¼ inch thick. Dice the potatoes into small irregular cubes. You should have about 2 cups.

2. Heat the butter and oil in a soup pot over medium-high heat. Add the scallions, give them a turn, and cook for a minute. Add the potatoes and 1 teaspoon salt and turn the heat down to medium. Cook for 4 to 5 minutes, stirring occasionally. When you get a whiff that says "home fries," add 6 cups water, bring to a boil, lower the heat, and simmer, covered, until the potatoes are soft, 20 to 30 minutes. Mash some of the potatoes against the side of the pot to give the soup a little more substance. Taste for salt and season with pepper.

3. Toss the tomatoes with the basil, shallot, and oil. Season with a pinch of sea salt or to taste. Ladle the soup into bowls, spoon some of the tomatoes and their juices into each portion, then serve.

Pepper and Tomato Soup
with noodles for late summer

MAKES ABOUT
2 QUARTS

Plump little nests of noodles give this vegetable soup the focus of a main dish. But with or without them, this soup is quite versatile, as the variations suggest.

You can make quite a good stock from the trimmings that accumulate as you work. But in simple soups such as this one, the quality of the ingredients is especially important—dense *ripe* tomatoes, *sweet* peppers, *sparkling* herbs.

2 large yellow or orange bell peppers
5 large ripe tomatoes
2 tablespoons fruity olive oil
$1\frac{1}{3}$ cups finely diced red onion
Pinch of saffron threads
Small handful of basil leaves, chopped
1 large garlic clove, minced with 6 parsley sprigs and $\frac{1}{4}$ teaspoon anise seeds
Sea salt and freshly ground pepper
1 heaping tablespoon tomato paste (sun-dried is good here)
1 teaspoon paprika
Opal basil leaves cut into thin strips, for garnish

2 eggs, separated
$1\frac{1}{2}$ cups fine egg noodles (fideos or linguine, broken into short pieces)
$\frac{1}{2}$ cup finely diced or grated fresh or regular mozzarella cheese
2 tablespoons chopped parsley
Peanut oil or light olive oil for frying

THE NOODLES

Once again a Provençal rosé would be the wine to serve with this herbaceous soup. Or try a Spanish rosé from the Navarra region with the smoky version.

1. Bring 6 cups water to a boil and add to it any trimmings produced by the vegetables, such as tomato skins and seeds, pepper cores, parsley and basil stems, plus perhaps a slice of onion, extra garlic, and so forth. Simmer while you prepare everything else. You'll be continuing to add trimmings to the stock as you work.

2. Roast the peppers directly over a flame or under a broiler until blistered and lightly charred. Put them in a bowl, cover, and set aside. Next roast the tomatoes in the flame, holding them in a pair of tongs, until blistered and cracked. Set them on a cutting board, peel off the skin, and add it to the stock. Halve them crosswise and squeeze the seeds into a strainer set over a bowl to catch the juice. Dice the walls into neat pieces and mince the cores. Add the seeds to the stock. Returning to the peppers, wipe off the charred skin, cut off the tops near the stem, and add them to the stock, as well as the cores and their seeds. Dice the peppers into small pieces.

3. Heat the oil in a wide soup pot over medium heat. Add the onion and crumble in the saffron threads. After a few minutes, add the basil, garlic, peppers, and 1 teaspoon salt. After 5 minutes more, stir in the tomato paste, paprika, diced tomatoes, and strained juice from the tomatoes. Strain the stock right into the pot as well and bring to a boil. Reduce the heat and simmer, covered, for 20 minutes.

4. While the soup is cooking, make the noodle cakes. Beat the egg whites until they hold stiff peaks, then stir in the yolks, noodles, cheese, and parsley. Season with a few pinches of salt, then work the mixture with your hands so that it's more or less homogenous. It will be stiff. Heat enough oil in a medium skillet to float the noodles, at least 1/3 inch deep—about a cup. When it's hot, drop the batter into the oil, dividing it into 6 roundish portions by eye. Fry until golden, then turn and fry the second side, about 2 minutes in all, depending on how hot your oil is. Set aside on paper towels to drain.

5. Just before serving, reheat the soup, add the noodle cakes, and simmer for 10 minutes. Season with pepper and opal basil and serve.

- *With Goat Cheese Crostini:* In place of the noodle nests, toast a baguette slice for each bowl, spread with goat cheese, and float one in each bowl of soup.
- *A Smoky Version:* Add ½ teaspoon or more to taste Spanish smoked paprika (page 92) to the onion.
- *A Smooth Version:* Puree the soup until smooth. Serve seasoned with a few drops of sherry vinegar. Finely slivered cabbage (Napa, Savoy, green) added at the end is delicious here and gives the soup some texture.
- *Chilled:* Omit making the noodle nests in this version. Chill the soup and serve it with a few drops of vinegar in each bowl, diced avocado, or a dollop of saffron mayonnaise.

Summer Squash in Broth
with masa dumplings and cilantro salsa

SERVES 6

This main-course vegetable soup is pretty with its summer squash in a Mexican-flavored tomato broth, cilantro pesto, and the bite-sized masa dumplings. It's more of a production than most soups because you need to make the broth, which you can assemble in just a few moments though it wants two hours on the stove, the dumplings, *and* the salsa. But no one part is complicated or difficult—it just has to be done. The masa dumplings can be made hours ahead of time.

Start the broth first if you haven't any on hand. Make the dumplings while the broth is cooking, followed by the salsa. Complete the soup just before you serve it because its success depends in part on the vegetables being *just* done and the cilantro salsa vibrant and green.

THE MASA DUMPLINGS
½ cup masa harina
½ cup all-purpose flour
1 teaspoon baking powder
1 tablespoon ground pure red chile (not chili powder)
⅜ teaspoon salt
1 tablespoon chopped oregano or 1 teaspoon dried
½ cup grated Jack cheese
1 large egg

2 tablespoons melted butter or canola oil, plus oil for frying

⅓ cup milk or water

THE CILANTRO SALSA

1 cup coarsely chopped cilantro

1 jalapeño chile, seeded and finely diced

2 tablespoons olive oil

Sea salt

THE SOUP

6 cups Mexican Tomato Broth (page 29)

3 ripe tomatoes or a handful of cherry tomatoes, cut into bite-sized pieces

3 cups thinly sliced small squash: zucchini, pattypan, or a mixture

3 scallions, white parts plus some green, thinly sliced

1 avocado

1 lime, cut in 6 wedges

1. To make the dumplings, stir the masa, flour, baking powder, chile, salt, and oregano together with a fork to blend, then toss in the cheese. Beat the egg with the butter and milk, pour it into the masa, and stir with a fork to bring the dough together, then use your hands to gently form it into a solid mass. Break off small pieces of dough and roll them into marbles. Heat ¼ inch vegetable oil in a skillet. When hot, add the masa balls and cook for several minutes, shaking them around the pan, until golden, then remove and set aside on paper towels.

2. Make the salsa by mixing together the cilantro, chile, oil, and a little water, if needed to thin it out a bit. You can leave it with some texture or puree until smooth. Season with salt.

3. To make the soup, heat the broth. Divide the tomatoes among the serving bowls. Simmer the squash and scallions in the broth for 5 minutes, then add the dumplings and cook for 4 or 5 minutes longer. Spoon the vegetables and dumplings over the tomatoes, then pour on the broth. Slice the avocado into the soup, add a dollop of the cilantro salsa, and serve with the lime wedges.

A Farmers' Market Soup
with pasta and pesto

I love *soupe au pistou,* that bounteous collection of simmered summer vegetables and beans finished with pesto. But since I don't necessarily want to be cooking dried beans at the peak of the summer's heat and canned beans are too soft, pasta takes their place.

This is just the kind of seasonal dish that shows how much flavor comes from the garden, for it's only that and not some difficult technique that accounts for its goodness. If I'm a bit loose on measurements, it's because sizes and varieties vary in true garden or farmers' market vegetables. I don't think there's really some exact formulation to follow. Even if I use all these vegetables every time, I never end up with the same soup twice.

3 tablespoons olive oil

3 leeks, white parts plus an inch of green, chopped and rinsed

Pinch of saffron threads

3 medium to large carrots, diced

3 yellow waxy boiling potatoes, chopped

3 medium turnips, peeled and diced

3 zucchini or other summer squash, sliced into ½-inch rounds or chunks

¾ pound green beans, tipped, tailed, and cut into 1-inch lengths

2 large ripe tomatoes, any color, peeled, seeded, and diced

2 garlic cloves, minced

Sea salt and freshly ground pepper

2 quarts vegetable stock made with summer vegetables (page 10) or water

1 cup dried pasta: pastini, orzo, broken spaghetti, or other small shapes

THE PESTO   3 cups loosely packed basil leaves, stems removed

1 plump garlic clove, peeled

3 tablespoons pine nuts

½ cup freshly grated Parmigiano-Reggiano

2 tablespoons grated pecorino Romano

½ cup extra virgin olive oil

I blanch the basil in boiling water before working it into a sauce. The reason is because our basil is very mature and even tough, making the leaves difficult to pound or puree without bruising them. In Liguria, the home of pesto, basil is butter-soft and easy to work into a pesto. The plants are about the size we buy for transplanting.

We like this summer vegetable soup with Bonny Doon's Vin Gris de Cigare rosé, a spicy, refreshing, summertime wine.

1. Warm the oil in a wide soup pot over medium heat. Add the leeks and saffron and cook gently until the leeks look glossy and translucent and the saffron begins to release its aroma, about 10 minutes. Add the vegetables, including the juice from the tomatoes, the garlic, and $1\frac{1}{2}$ teaspoons salt. Cook for 5 minutes more, then add the stock. Bring to a boil, lower the heat, and simmer until the vegetables are tender, 20 to 30 minutes.

2. Meanwhile, cook the pasta in salted boiling water, then drain and rinse under cold water to stop the cooking.

3. Make the pesto. Drop the basil into boiling water for a second or two, then drain, rinse, and pat dry. Mash the garlic in a mortar with $\frac{1}{4}$ teaspoon salt and the pine nuts, then add the basil leaves a handful at a time. Grind them, using a circular motion, until you have a fairly fine paste with very small flecks of leaves. Briefly work in the cheeses, then stir in the olive oil. Taste for salt. Or, to use a food processor, process the garlic, salt, and pine nuts until finely chopped, then add the basil and olive oil and puree until smooth. Add the cheeses and process just to combine.

4. Add the pasta to the hot soup, then ladle the soup into bowls and stir a spoonful of pesto into each serving. Season with pepper. The soup need not be piping hot. In fact, it's better served a little more on the tepid side.

A Smoky One—Tomato Bisque

One magnificent, giant Brandywine tomato that needed to be used right away tempted me to turn it into a soup, just to see how far a one-pound tomato would go. It made a serving for one. In fact, tomatoes generally do work out as a pound to a cup, whether soup or sauce, and when it comes to this recipe, it can easily be multiplied to make more.

2 teaspoons olive oil
$\frac{1}{4}$ onion, thinly sliced (about $\frac{1}{2}$ cup)
1 garlic clove, slivered
$\frac{1}{4}$ teaspoon Spanish smoked paprika (page 92), or more to taste
One 1-pound ripe low-acid tomato or 1 pound smaller tomatoes, cut into chunks
1 slice sturdy bread, torn into pieces
1 thyme, marjoram, or basil sprig
Sea salt and freshly ground pepper
$\frac{1}{4}$ teaspoon sugar
1 tablespoon cream

Tiny bread cubes
Olive oil for frying
Pinch of minced parsley and thyme leaves

1. Warm the oil in a saucepan, then add the onion and garlic. Cook for 3 minutes, then add the paprika, toss in the tomato, bread, herbs, $\frac{1}{4}$ teaspoon each salt and sugar, and 1 cup water. Bring to a boil, cover the pot, then lower the heat and simmer until the tomato has broken down, about 20 minutes.

2. Pass the soup through a food mill, pressing out all the juices you can. Return it to the stove, taste for salt, and season with pepper. If you want more smokiness, add more paprika, a pinch at a time.

3. Stir in the cream. Crisp the bread cubes in a little olive oil over medium-low heat until golden, 6 to 8 minutes. Add the croutons and herbs and serve.

For wine, try a lighter-bodied Zinfandel or Primativo from Puglia.

Iced Tomato Soup
in three colors

Once you have good tomatoes in hand, nothing is faster to make than this chilled soup. It's seasoned simply with salt, tasty olive oil, fresh lemon, and herbs, and if you want to have it right away, you can add a few ice cubes to each batch when you blend it. Use different kinds of tomatoes to make red, yellow, and green soups. Pour them into chilled glasses, one type of tomato to a glass or some of each color in layers. If you want texture, peel, seed, and dice some extra tomato and add it to each glass.

2 red, 2 yellow, and 2 (or more, because they're often smallish) green zebra
    tomatoes
Sea salt and freshly ground pepper
Fresh lemon juice or vinegar to taste
Extra virgin olive oil to taste
Minced opal basil, marjoram, lemon basil, dill, or lovage

Puree each color tomato separately in a blender until smooth. Chill well, then season each batch to taste with salt, lemon juice or vinegar, and olive oil, using about a teaspoon of oil per serving. Pour the purees into chilled glasses, one type to a glass or in separate layers, and garnish with the fresh herbs and freshly ground pepper.

White Gazpacho
of almonds and melon (ajo blanco)

A silky texture and the presence of garlic, salt, and the melon (or large green grapes) make a concoction that's at once sweet, salty, and pungent. The first time I had this, in Spain, I was immediately reminded of those perfumed Arab almond-

based drinks scented with orange-flower water, to which this is related. Both are luxurious given the quantity of nuts and the labor of pounding and straining, even if that is now done by a food processor. Because this is a rich soup, it can be served in quite small portions; this amount will serve six or more.

1 large slice white country bread or baguette
¾ cup almonds
2 garlic cloves, not too large, peeled
Sea salt
1 tablespoon sherry vinegar, plus extra to taste
6 tablespoons olive oil, preferably Spanish
2 cups ice water
2 cups diced fragrant green melon, such as Galia or Passport, or 24 large seedless green grapes, peeled and halved

1. Put the bread on a plate, drizzle several tablespoons of water over it, and set aside.

2. Bring several cups of water to a boil, add the almonds, turn off the heat, and let stand for 1 minute. Drain, then rinse with cold water. Pinch off the skins with your fingers.

This rich soup wants some bubbles to contrast with its creaminess. A Spanish cava would be an obvious and good choice.

3. Grind the almonds in a food processor with the garlic and ½ teaspoon salt until reduced to fine crumbs. Add the bread and vinegar and continue working until it is as smooth as possible. It may clump together, but you can't overwork it. With the machine running, slowly pour in the oil, followed by the ice water. Be sure to scrape down the sides as the ground almonds can stick to them. Pour the soup through a fine strainer set over a bowl, and gently press the liquid out with a rubber scraper so that the soup is silky smooth. Discard the solids and refrigerate the soup until it's good and cold, 2 to 3 hours. Taste for salt and vinegar. The sharpness of the vinegar should be just detectable.

4. Serve small portions of the soup, dividing the melon or grapes among them.

Fall is a great season for roasted vegetable soups. First of all, roasting intensifies their flavors. But another reason to make roasted vegetable soups at this time of year is that while it starts to get nippy out, the days end up too warm to warrant turning on the heat. What better way, then, to cut the morning's chill than to turn on the oven and roast vegetables for a soup, even if you finish making it later?

Fall vegetables are still mostly moisture filled—tomatoes, peppers, and eggplant. Even the first winter squashes of the season contain quite a bit of water. Roasting pulls out that moisture and evaporates it, leaving behind the sugars and concentrating the flavors of the vegetables. Thus, soups based on roasted vegetables tend to have richer flavors than if the vegetables were merely simmered in water or stock.

They also tend to be pureed soups, because well-roasted vegetables tend to shrivel and even blacken in places. In other words, they're not so pretty to look at. But a few of them pulled from the roasting pan and diced can make a great textured addition to a pureed soup.

In general, it seems to take about one and a half hours at 375 to 425 degrees to

sufficiently roast soup vegetables so that they get that special flavor. Toss them with olive or other appropriate oil so they don't become completely desiccated. The oil coating serves to create a good balance between water lost and flavor gained.

Roasted Carrot Soup

MAKES ABOUT
6 CUPS

When you notice that carrots are suddenly really delicious, keep this soup in mind. A robust soup is easier to produce if the carrots are sweet to start with. It's finished with just a little minced parsley and a swirl of crème fraîche.

1 pound carrots, cut into chunks

2 small potatoes, cut into chunks

1 large onion, cut into chunks

5 garlic cloves, peeled

2 to 4 tablespoons olive oil

Sea salt and freshly ground pepper

2 hefty thyme sprigs

1 bay leaf

1 quart Vegetable Stock (page 13) or water

½ cup light cream

2 to 3 tablespoons crème fraîche or sour cream, stirred with a fork until loosened

2 teaspoons minced parsley

1. Preheat the oven to 425°F. Toss the vegetables with the olive oil and season with ½ teaspoon salt and some pepper. Put them in a large baking dish with the thyme and bay leaf and roast until tender and glazed, about 1 hour, turning them 2 or 3 times.

2. Transfer the vegetables to a soup pot, add the stock, and bring to a boil. Simmer until the carrots are soft, about 20 minutes, then puree until smooth. Return the puree to the pot, taste for salt, and season with pepper. Stir in the cream.

3. Ladle the soup into bowls, swirl a spoonful of crème fraîche into each, add a little minced parsley, and serve.

A fruit-forward Beaujolais is just the wine to ease into fall with this carrot soup.

roasted vegetable soups for fall

Roasted Eggplant and Pepper Soup
with ginger, cumin, and yogurt

This soup can be served hot, tepid, or chilled—its flavors perhaps optimal at room temperature. It won't win any beauty contests—eggplant makes everything a bit dull looking—but leaving some texture in the soup helps, along with the swirl of yogurt and a perfect sprig or two of cilantro. In any case, the flavors will win kudos, and that's what counts.

1 pound eggplant, preferably small lighter-skinned varieties
2 red bell peppers
1 large onion
4 tomatoes (about 1 pound)
5 plump garlic cloves, peeled
2 thyme and oregano sprigs, or a couple pinches of *each* dried
1/4 cup olive oil
Sea salt
1 teaspoon ground roasted cumin seeds
6 thin slices peeled ginger
3 tablespoons minced cilantro stems
Juice of 1 large lime
1 cup yogurt, such as Pavels, a thin whole-milk yogurt

A lighter crianza-style Rioja will provide the acidity and fruit needed to balance the smooth texture and spice of this soup.

1. Preheat the oven to 425°F. Cut the eggplant, peppers, onion, and tomatoes into large chunks and put them in a large baking dish with the garlic. Toss with the herbs, oil, and 3/4 teaspoon salt. Roast the vegetables until browned and fragrant, about 1 hour, turning them 2 or 3 times while they're roasting.

2. Transfer the vegetables to a soup pot. Add 1 cup water to the pan they baked in, scrape up the caramelized juices, and add to the pot along with the cumin and ginger. Pour in another 6 cups water, the cilantro, and 1/2 teaspoon salt. Bring to a boil, then lower the heat and simmer, covered, until the vegetables are fully tender, 20 minutes or so. Let cool slightly, then puree, leaving a little texture. Add

the lime juice, then stir in the yogurt, leaving it swirled rather than blended. Serve garnished with sprigs of cilantro.

If you don't care for pureed soups, and not everyone does, take a little extra time to cut the vegetables into pieces not too big for a soupspoon. Make the soup as directed, but puree just a cupful or so to unify the background while maintaining the shapes and colors of the vegetables.

A Visual Variation

Roasted Jerusalem Artichoke Bisque
with sunflower sprouts

MAKES 7 TO 8 CUPS

These knobby tubers, which grow in copious amounts, are in the sunflower family, so I like to keep them with their relatives, using sunflower seed oil for roasting and nutty-flavored sunflower sprouts as a fresh garnish. For a soup with such humble beginnings, this ends up quite elegant.

1 pound Jerusalem artichokes, scrubbed and cut into $\frac{1}{3}$-inch slices
3 ounces potato, peeled and sliced (about $\frac{1}{2}$ cup)
3 large garlic cloves
3 tablespoons sunflower seed oil
Sea salt and freshly ground pepper
1 small onion or leek, thinly sliced
$\frac{1}{4}$ cup cream
Handful of sunflower seed sprouts

1. Preheat the oven to 425°F. Toss the Jerusalem artichokes, potato, and unpeeled garlic cloves with 2 tablespoons of the oil and a few pinches of salt. Put them in a 9 × 12-inch baking dish and roast for 45 minutes, or until the tubers are browned in places.

For wine, try a fruit-forward Chardonnay, such as one from Sonoma's Russian River Valley.

roasted vegetable soups for fall

Roasted Jerusalem Artichoke
Bisque with Sunflower Sprouts

2. Heat the remaining tablespoon of oil in a soup pot and add the onion. Cook over medium heat, stirring occasionally, for several minutes, then add the roasted vegetables, $\frac{1}{2}$ teaspoon salt, and $\frac{1}{2}$ cup water. Cook over medium heat, stirring occasionally, for 4 to 5 minutes, then add $4\frac{1}{2}$ cups water and scrape any browned juices from the pan. Reduce the heat and simmer, covered, until the vegetables are soft, about 20 minutes.

3. Puree the soup, leaving a bit of texture and flecks of brown from the Jerusalem artichokes. Stir in the cream, taste for salt, and season with pepper. Serve garnished with a lofty pile of the fleshy sprouts in each bowl.

Roasted Turnip Soup
with caramelized turnips

MAKES 6 CUPS

If you want to warm your kitchen for an hour or so on a cold day, turn on the oven and roast these turnips until caramelized. Once they're browned, add milk and water, and you'll have a beautiful soup in about twenty-five minutes, finished with "croutons" of caramelized turnips and tarragon.

Lovely tender turnips with their greens needn't be peeled. If you're using storage turnips, peel them thickly before dicing and parboil them for three minutes.

$1\frac{1}{2}$ pounds turnips

1 large onion, cut into large pieces

4 large garlic cloves, peeled

2 thyme sprigs or $\frac{1}{2}$ teaspoon dried

2 tablespoons olive or sunflower seed oil

Sea salt and freshly ground pepper

2 cups milk

TO FINISH

1 to 2 tablespoons butter

1 or 2 pinches of sugar

2 teaspoons minced tarragon

For wine, try a low-alcohol Italian white, such as an Orvieto, with these sweet roasted turnips.

1. Preheat the oven to 425°F. Peel the turnips, then chunk two-thirds of them into roughly 1-inch pieces. Set the remainder aside. Simmer storage turnips in boiling salted water for 3 minutes, then drain. Fresh turnips (those with their greens) needn't be parboiled.

2. Toss the turnip chunks with the onion, garlic, thyme, oil, and ½ teaspoon salt, then put them in a large baking dish in a single layer. Bake for 45 minutes to an hour, shuffling the vegetables every 15 minutes so that they brown on all sides. Transfer to a soup pot. Add ½ cup water to the roasting pan, scrape up the caramelized juices, and pour them into the pot.

3. Season with ½ teaspoon salt, add the milk and 2 cups water to the vegetables, and bring to a boil. Lower the heat and simmer, covered, until the turnips are tender, 20 to 25 minutes. Puree until smooth and return to the pot. Season with salt to taste. The soup can be made ahead to this point.

4. To finish, dice the remaining turnips into ½-inch cubes. Melt the butter in a small skillet, add the turnips, sprinkle with sugar, and cook over medium heat until golden, about 15 minutes. Season with salt and pepper and stir in most of the tarragon. Ladle the soup into bowls, spoon the caramelized turnips into each one, garnish with the remaining tarragon, and serve.

MAKES ABOUT
2 QUARTS

Roasted Butternut Squash Soup
with seared radicchio and pumpkin seed oil

Nutty-tasting, slightly bitter radicchio makes a good match for the sweet squash, while the motor-oil-dark-green Austrian pumpkin seed oil, truly redolent of that vegetable, is the natural enhancement for this, or any squash- or pumpkin-based, soup. But if you can't find any, leave it out or finish the soup with a little extra virgin olive oil and the shavings of Parmigiano-Reggiano cheese.

THE SOUP

2½ to 3 pounds butternut squash

2 to 3 tablespoons olive oil, plus extra for the squash

2 onions, finely chopped

10 sage leaves, chopped, or ½ teaspoon dried

3 thyme sprigs, leaves stripped and chopped, or ¼ teaspoon dried

¼ cup chopped parsley

2 garlic cloves, finely chopped

Sea salt and freshly ground pepper

2 quarts vegetable stock (see sidebar) or water

TO FINISH

2 tablespoons olive oil

1 head of radicchio, cut into wedges 1 to 2 inches wide at the center

1 teaspoon balsamic vinegar

Pumpkin seed oil or extra virgin olive oil, a few drops per bowl

Thin shavings of Parmigiano-Reggiano

You can use any kind of squash or pumpkin here (page 172), but I've called for butternut since it is so available, so easy to use, and reliably good. As for stock, you can skip it or simmer squash seeds and fibers with some sliced onion, parsley, garlic, and thyme for twenty-five minutes.

1. Preheat the oven to 425°F. Halve the squash and scoop out the seeds, then brush the surfaces with oil. Place the halves cut side down on a baking sheet or gratin dish and bake until tender when pressed with a finger, about 30 minutes. Scoop out the flesh, making sure to include any caramelized bits. Deglaze the pan with 1 cup water and reserve.

With this soup we're moving into cooler weather, time for a fruity cool-climate Pinot Noir from New Zealand.

2. Heat the oil in a soup pot. Add the onions, sage, thyme, and parsley and cook over medium heat, stirring frequently, until the onions have begun to brown around the edges, about 15 minutes. Add the cooked squash, garlic, 1½ teaspoons salt, and the stock plus deglazing water. Bring to a boil, then lower the heat and simmer, partially covered, for 25 minutes. If the soup becomes too thick, add more water to thin it out. Taste for salt. Puree until the soup is silky smooth or, if you prefer, leave a bit more texture.

3. To finish, heat a cast-iron skillet over medium-high heat and add a tablespoon of oil. When hot, add the radicchio, pressing the wedges into the pan. Season them with salt and pepper and brush with the remaining oil. When the leaves have browned, after 4 to 5 minutes, turn the radicchio over and brown the second side. Remove from the heat and sprinkle with the vinegar. Chop the leaves into bite-sized pieces.

4. To serve, ladle the hot soup into soup plates, add the radicchio, and drizzle a few drops of pumpkin seed oil—or fine olive oil—into each bowl. Shave a little Parmesan into each bowl, add cracked pepper, and serve.

Roasted Squash, Pear, and Ginger Soup

MAKES ABOUT
4½ CUPS

Roasting the squash in chunks, with its skin on, gives us a way to use some of the more interesting but otherwise hard-to-access varieties. You don't need to make a stock, but the possibilities the roasted skins and squash seeds hold for extra flavor make it worth simmering them for twenty-five minutes in water once you've scraped off the cooked flesh.

This fall soup is like putting on the first sweater of the season: it just feels so good. Although the soup takes several steps—roasting the squash and pears (which can be done a day ahead of time), cooking them, and finally pureeing the soup—none involve much from you. It's an easily made soup that will keep well for days—a great possibility for a holiday meal.

One 2½-pound Buttercup, Perfection, or other dense winter squash, rinsed
3 ripe but firm pears, any variety, quartered, seeds and stems removed
1 chunk fresh ginger, about 2 inches long, thinly sliced
Sunflower seed or olive oil for the squash
Sea salt
2 tablespoons butter or sunflower seed oil
1 onion, thinly sliced
½ cup crème fraîche or sour cream, optional

1. Preheat the oven to 425°F. Cut the squash in half, scrape out the seeds, then cut each half into thirds. Put the pieces in a large baking dish or roasting pan with the pears and all but a few slices of the ginger. Brush with oil, season with salt, and

For wine, turn to a heartier white with bright tropical fruit, such as Sanford's Chardonnay from Santa Barbara County.

bake until fragrant and tender, about 1 hour. Turn the pieces once or twice so that they have a chance to caramelize on more than one surface. If the squash seems very dry (some varieties are), add 1 cup water to the pan to create steam and cover with foil. When the squash is tender, transfer everything from the pan to a cutting board, add 1 cup water to the pan, and scrape to dissolve the juices, reserving the liquid. Scrape the flesh of the squash away from the skins. You should have about 2 cups.

2. To make a stock, bring 6 cups water to a boil and add the seeds and, eventually, the squash skins, the remaining ginger, and ½ teaspoon salt. Lower the heat and simmer, covered, for 20 to 25 minutes.

3. Meanwhile, melt the butter in a soup pot. Add the onion, give it a stir, and cook over medium-low heat, stirring frequently, until it begins to brown a bit and is fragrant, about 10 minutes. Add the pears, ginger, and squash, then the reserved deglazing water. Strain the stock into the pot. Bring to a boil, then lower the heat and simmer, covered, for 25 minutes. Cool briefly, then puree until smooth and pass through a food mill or strainer to ensure a silky texture. Serve as is or swirl in the crème fraîche.

Three Variations

- Dice a pear or an apple, sprinkle with a little sugar, and caramelize in a little butter or oil. Use these "croutons" as a finishing touch.
- Omit the ginger and add cooked wild rice to the finished soup.
- Crisp thin strips of fresh ginger in oil or butter and add a cluster to each serving.

Roasted Fall Tomato Soup
with saffron quinoa

There's always a time in October when you can be sipping an iced tomato soup one day while looking forward the next to turning on the oven for this roasted tomato soup. When the first hard frost is close, pick the last of your ripe tomatoes and make this warming soup. And if the weather changes back to summer, know that you can serve this chilled instead.

The roasting takes about an hour, the finishing a matter of minutes. Have a food mill on hand for the best texture.

roasted vegetable soups for fall

Quinoa cooked in saffron-stained water provides this soup with the welcome texture that pureed soups lack. And it looks very pretty with its tiny golden pearls peppering the deep red tomato.

3 tablespoons olive or sunflower seed oil

1 onion, sliced

3 pounds ripe late-summer red or black-skinned tomatoes, rinsed and halved

Sea salt and freshly ground pepper

1 tablespoon agave syrup (page 140) or brown sugar, or more to taste

2 garlic cloves, slivered

1 pinch of saffron threads

½ cup quinoa, rinsed well in cool water

1 to 2 teaspoons curry powder, to taste

TO FINISH

½ cup yogurt, whisked until smooth

Minced serrano or jalapeño chile

Chopped cilantro

The curry and saffron call for a spicy lighter-style Zinfandel from Sonoma County, such as Rafanelli.

1. Preheat the oven to 375°F. Brush some of the oil over a 9 × 12-inch baking dish, scatter the onion over that, then add the tomatoes, cut side up. Sprinkle with 1 teaspoon salt, plenty of pepper, and the syrup. Slip the garlic into the tomatoes. Drizzle with the remaining oil and bake for 1 hour.

2. Bring 1 cup water to a boil with the saffron and ¼ teaspoon salt. Add the quinoa, reduce the heat to low, then cover and cook until the grains have absorbed the water and the germ is visible, about 15 minutes. Set aside.

3. Puree the tomatoes with their juices, then pass them through a food mill or strainer. Stir in curry powder, hold backing a little if the soup is going to stand for a day. Season with more salt and syrup if needed.

4. Ladle the soup into bowls, divide the quinoa among them, swirl in a spoonful of yogurt, and garnish with the minced chile and/or cilantro.

Silky Roasted Yellow Pepper Soup

When visiting the North Farmers' Market in Columbus one late September, I happily filled a bag with huge golden peppers to take home with me. Among the last vegetables to ripen, these peppers are a treat, and I wanted to use them to make this soup. It's a little laborious to make, but you don't need to serve a lot of it—just a taste at the start of the meal. And there are many ways you can finish this soup—with a vinegar reduction, romesco sauce spread on small croutons, sour cream and chives, a salsa verde (see page 142), or the garnish of tiny minced peppers shown here. And you can serve it hot or chilled.

THE STOCK

2 teaspoons olive oil

1 small onion, sliced

Cores and trimmings from the peppers

1 small zucchini, chopped

1 small carrot, chopped

Handful of ripe small tomatoes or a large tomato, halved

Few basil leaves

1 thyme sprig or pinch of dried

Sea salt

THE SOUP

2 pounds (4 to 5) meaty yellow bell peppers, tops sliced off, cores and seeds
　　reserved for stock

Olive oil as needed

1 small red onion, thinly sliced (about 1 cup)

Vinegar (such as Chardonnay, sherry, or balsamic) to taste

2 tablespoons finely diced bell pepper, different colors

1. Preheat the broiler and position a rack about 8 inches beneath the broiling unit. Begin the stock: Heat the oil in a pot over medium-high heat and add the onion and the rest of the ingredients as you slice them, along with a scant teaspoon salt. When the onion has some color, after about 5 minutes, add 5 cups water, bring to

You *can* quickly throw together a pepper soup if you don't bother to peel or roast the peppers. Just sauté them with the onions, add water or stock, and you're done. However, it's the skins that give peppers a sharp taste, so I take extra time to broil then peel the peppers. While the broiler is heating, I use the pepper cores and a few fall vegetables to make a simple, flavor-enhancing stock.

a boil, then lower the heat and simmer, partially covered, for about 25 minutes. Strain.

An interesting wine choice would be a California Rhône-inspired white, such as Qupé's Marsanne or Roussanne.

2. Cut the peppers in half lengthwise and flatten them. Brush the skins with oil, including the tops (minus their stems), and place them skin side up on a sheet pan. Broil only until the skin is bubbling, puckered, and lightly browned, about 12 minutes. Put them in a bowl, cover, and leave them to steam for at least 15 minutes.

3. Meanwhile, heat 1½ tablespoons oil in a soup pot. Add the onion and cook over low heat while you peel the peppers. Pull or scrape off as much skin as you can without making yourself crazy, then chop the peppers and add them to the pot as you go, along with ½ teaspoon salt and the strained stock. Bring to a boil and simmer, covered, for 20 minutes. Cool slightly, then puree in batches. For the best texture, pass the soup through a food mill. Taste for salt and add a few drops of vinegar to bring everything together. Serve with a spoonful of the diced pepper in each bowl or another garnish (see headnote).

Hearty Mushroom Broth
with roasted vegetables
(a vegetable pot-au-feu)

SERVES 4

In addition to roasted vegetables, this broth-based soup might include some steamed ones, such as wedges of Savoy cabbage or Brussels sprouts. In fact, I rather like the contrast of roasted with steamed. What's important is to cut everything beautifully. Other vegetables to consider using are spears or chunks of sweet potatoes, celery root, celery, and parsnips.

The mushroom broth requires some cooking time, but it's so good that I make it often and keep bags of it in the freezer to pull out at will. That alone makes this soup far easier to put together than if you're starting everything from scratch.

A lighter-style French Pinot Noir from the Côte Chalonnaise takes this soup into fall and early winter.

8 small carrots, peeled and diagonally or roll-cut into long pieces

8 small turnips, peeled and cut into 1-inch wedges

6 small potatoes, peeled and cut into 1-inch chunks or wedges

3 or more portobello mushrooms, stems removed, gills scraped, halved

Olive oil as needed

Sea salt and freshly ground pepper

3 thyme sprigs

1 bay leaf

¾ cup white wine or sake

4 to 6 cups Hearty Mushroom Broth (page 34)

4 cabbage wedges, 1 inch thick, or 12 Brussels sprouts, halved

1. Preheat the oven to 425°F. Toss the vegetables with olive oil to coat them lightly and season with salt and pepper. Put them in a wide baking dish, add the herbs, pour in the wine, and cover with foil. Bake for 15 minutes, then remove the foil, shuffle the pan, and continue baking until the vegetables are browned and tender, another 30 minutes or so. Check them as they cook and remove any that are clearly done.

2. Puree the broth with about ¼ cup carrot for each cup of broth until smooth, to give it more body.

3. Steam the cabbage wedges until tender, about 10 minutes. Pour the broth into heated soup plates, arrange the vegetables in an attractive manner, and serve.

Tender dumplings make this even more stewlike and filling. Cook them separately in water so that they don't drink up all the broth, then add them to the pot-au-feu. You can make one large one for each bowl or many smaller ones. In either case, you might not want to use all the batter—it will make more than what's needed for 4 servings, but it's hard to make in smaller amounts.

1 cup flour
1 teaspoon baking powder
Sea salt and freshly ground pepper
$^3/_4$ cup milk, heated with 3 tablespoons butter or oil
1 heaping tablespoon finely minced rosemary
1 large egg

1. Mix the flour with the baking powder, $^3/_8$ teaspoon salt, and a few grindings of pepper. Pour in the milk, rosemary, and egg and stir quickly together with a fork.

2. Bring a wide skillet of water to a boil and add salt to taste, then reduce the heat to a simmer. Drop in the dumplings by spoonfuls, making them large or small as you wish. Cover and cook until they're puffed and firm, about 10 minutes. Divide them among the soup plates.

For a sort of East-West soup, season the broth with red or white miso, adding a tablespoon (or more). Cut a block of firm tofu into triangles, brown in a tiny bit of oil on both sides, then add them to the barely simmering broth and cook until heated through. Include any other vegetables that strike your fancy, from rounds of leeks and lotus root to steamed slivers of baby bok choy to the roasted vegetables. Finish with a few drops of roasted sesame oil in each bowl.

*A*lthough it's true that soups are good at any time of year, winter is their season more than any other. A warming bowl of soup is just the thing to turn a chilled soul into a warmer, happier person. Physically, this happens from the inside out. But soup can also warm us from the outside in. Think of serving winter soups in bowls that you can pick up and hold. Solid bowls of easy round shapes are ideal for this, as are mugs. Delicate porcelain has its place at the table, but there's nothing like holding a warm bowl on a chilly day and feeling your hands and heart thaw.

This chapter is devoted to soups that feature winter vegetables—roots and tubers, onions, squashes, some greens, and canned tomatoes. But there are a great many more soups that are ideal for this season, particularly those that are thickened with bread and grains or made from beans and lentils. Still, the vegetable option is appealing and important in winter. It's a time when the produce we have not only is limited but takes longer to prepare than summer's tomatoes or spring's asparagus, and salads are perhaps less appealing than they are at other times of the year. Winter vegetable soups nicely fill the gap created by climate and choice.

Red Beet Soup
with beets and their greens

The stock uses the
trimmings of the soup
vegetables, so you are
basically doing your
soup prep as you
make the stock,
adding trimmings as
you go. As for the
pepper, I think it's
better if you can peel
it, especially if the
skin is waxed. Peeled,
it won't have any
skins that will roll up
into little scrolls.

This gorgeous beet soup uses the whole vegetable—roots, stems, and leaves. In spite of their earthy and even aggressive nature, I've found that beets don't make a hearty soup without the help of a stock and a strong supporting cast of vegetables. You'll do well to make a vegetable stock, which simply uses more of the vegetables that you're already using for the soup. Begin it first, and by the time you're ready to add it to the vegetables, it will be ready as well. A little lemon juice or apple cider vinegar brightens the flavors at the end, as does a dollop of sour cream or yogurt.

THE STOCK
1 tablespoon olive oil
1 cup leek greens and the roots, well washed
1 onion, sliced
1 carrot, chopped
1 celery rib, chopped
3 bay leaves
1 thyme sprig or pinch of dried
1 oregano branch or few pinches of dried
3 garlic cloves, smashed
Stems from 1 bunch of red beets
Handful of lentils
Sea salt

THE SOUP
1 tablespoon *each* olive oil and butter
3 small leeks, no more than an inch across, white parts only, sliced into rounds
1 onion, finely diced
2 thin carrots, thinly sliced
1 red bell pepper, peeled and diced
6 small beets, about 1½ ounces each, neatly peeled and cut into wedges a scant ½ inch wide
3 small bay leaves
½ teaspoon dried oregano

Pinch of ground allspice or anise seeds
1 teaspoon finely minced garlic
Sea salt and freshly ground pepper
1 tablespoon brown sugar
One 15-ounce can organic diced tomatoes, fire-roasted or plain

Beet greens, chopped
1 lemon, quartered, or a cruet of apple cider vinegar
Sour cream or yogurt to pass at the table

Try a California Syrah or Grenache-based wine from Ridge Vineyards with this soup.

1. To make the stock, heat the oil in a pot, add the leek greens and roots, onion, carrot, celery, herbs, and garlic. Give everything a stir and cook over high heat, stirring frequently, until the vegetables take on a little color. Add the rest of the stock ingredients, including 1 teaspoon salt and 6 cups water. Bring to a boil, then lower the heat and simmer gently for no longer than 30 minutes (it will go from red to brown at about that point). As you peel the beets, be sure to add the peels, along with any other vegetable trimmings, such as the ends and veins of the bell pepper, to the stock.

2. While the stock is cooking, heat the oil and butter in a wide soup pot. Add the soup vegetables, bay leaves, oregano, allspice, and garlic. Stir to coat, then cook over medium heat for 12 to 15 minutes. Add salt to taste, the brown sugar, and tomatoes with their juices. Strain the stock directly into the soup pot. Simmer, partially covered, until the beets are tender but not mushy, 20 to 25 minutes. Taste for salt and season with pepper.

3. Cook the beet greens in a little water with a pinch of salt until tender, 3 to 4 minutes, then drain. Ladle the soup into bowls and add a clump of greens to each. Serve with the lemon or vinegar on the side and pass sour cream or yogurt at the table.

Broccoli Rabe and White Bean Soup
with toasted whole wheat country bread and parmesan cheese

When I parboil broccoli rabe before sautéing it, I always come away feeling it's a pity not to use the liquid. So here it is, with the greens, lots of garlic, a bit of hot pepper, and cannellini beans—canned in this case. This soup is full of big, bold flavors, and it can be made literally in minutes. Served with an accompaniment of garlic-rubbed whole wheat toast, this soup is best eaten soon after it's made.

Big bunch of broccoli rabe
2 tablespoons olive oil, plus extra oil for finishing
1 onion, quartered and sliced crosswise
3 garlic cloves, 2 coarsely chopped, 1 halved
1 or 2 pinches of hot red pepper flakes
Sea salt
Chunk of Parmigiano-Reggiano cheese rind
One 15-ounce can organic cannellini beans
4 slices whole wheat country bread
½ cup freshly grated Parmigiano-Reggiano or Asiago cheese

1. Cut the bulk of the stems off the broccoli rabe, but don't discard them. Chop the leaves coarsely, wash them well, and set aside in a colander. Using a paring knife, pull the tough fibers off the stems, then chop them into small pieces.

2. Heat the oil in a wide soup pot. When hot, add the onion and cook over medium-high heat, stirring frequently, until softened, about 5 minutes. Add the chopped garlic and pepper flakes, cook for a minute or so longer, then add the greens and the stems. Season with 1 teaspoon salt, toss around the pan until wilted, then add 5 cups water and the chunk of cheese rind. Bring to a boil, then lower the heat to a simmer. Add the beans, simmer for 15 minutes, then taste for salt.

3. Toast the bread and rub it with the halved garlic clove. Unless you prefer to serve it on the side, break or cut it into pieces and lay them in the bottom of each bowl. Sprinkle a tablespoon of the grated cheese over the bread, then add the beans, broth, and greens. Thread a little oil into each serving and add the rest of the cheese.

Potato and Endive Chowder
over gruyère cheese toast

I have included an endive soup elsewhere among my recipes, but I present it again here, because so many people can't imagine that endive can be cooked. It can, and it's very good that way, revealing more of the characteristic nutty flavor that all chicories gain when cooked. Toasted bread covered with Gruyère cheese is buried under the finished dish, turning it into a chowdery one-bowl meal.

2 to 4 tablespoons butter
3 plump white Belgian endives, chopped into 1-inch pieces
3 large leeks, white parts only, finely chopped and rinsed (about 3 cups)
1 pound boiling or Yellow Finn potatoes, scrubbed well and chunked into 1-inch
    pieces
2 carrots, grated
Aromatics: 1 bay leaf, 4 thyme sprigs, 4 parsley branches
Sea salt and freshly ground pepper
$\frac{1}{2}$ cup light cream or milk
4 to 6 slices country bread
Thinly sliced Gruyère cheese to cover the bread
Minced parsley and/or thyme

1. Melt the butter in a wide, heavy soup pot and add the endives and leeks. Cook briskly over medium-high heat for several minutes, then add the potatoes, carrots,

and aromatics. Season with $1\frac{1}{2}$ teaspoons salt, lower the heat to medium, and cook the vegetables, turning them occasionally until they smell very aromatic and are browned in places, about 10 minutes.

2. Add 7 cups water and $1\frac{1}{2}$ teaspoons salt and bring to a boil. Lower the heat and simmer, partially covered, until the potatoes are soft, about 30 minutes. Press a few potatoes against the side of the pan to break them up and give the soup body. Add the cream, then taste for salt and season with pepper.

3. Toast the bread, lay the cheese over it, then set the toasts in soup plates. Ladle the chowder over the bread, sprinkle with parsley and/or thyme, and serve.

Pinot Noir is great with the potatoes and the cheese. One with balanced acidity, such as an Oregon Pinot, would be in order. Ideal would be a Ponzi Pinot from the Willamette Valley.

SERVES 4

Onion Soup
with red wine and tomatoes

Here's a French onion soup that doesn't depend on beef stock, for masses of red onions and red wine yield a robust soup. While you can simply serve it up in bowls with its bread and cheese, I prefer to finish this soup in a large round earthenware casserole set under the broiler until bubbly. It makes a grand presentation this way, one that is homey yet out of the ordinary.

2 tablespoons butter or olive oil

6 large red onions, quartered and sliced crosswise (about 3 pounds)

Sea salt and freshly ground pepper

Several thyme sprigs or $\frac{1}{8}$ teaspoon dried

2 bay leaves

2 cloves

4 parsley branches

2 teaspoons minced rosemary

1 tablespoon tomato paste

1 to 2 cups full-bodied red wine
1 cup ground or finely chopped tomatoes (such as Pomi)

8 diagonal baguette slices
1 cup grated Gruyère cheese
⅓ cup freshly grated Parmigiano-Reggiano

1. Melt the butter in a wide soup pot. Add the onions and 1 teaspoon salt, the herbs, and the spices and cook, covered, over low heat, stirring occasionally, until the liquid released by the onions has evaporated, about 30 minutes. Toward the end you need to be near the pot and stir it frequently. Cook until the onions are very soft and a glaze has built up on the pot.

Even without the traditional beef broth, this soup could be served with a bright California Pinot Noir such as Arcadian, from Santa Barbara.

2. Stir in the tomato paste, then pour in the wine, scrape the pot, raise the heat, and cook until the wine has bubbled away, about 5 minutes. Add the tomatoes and 1 quart water. Bring to a boil, then lower the heat and simmer, covered, for 20 minutes. Remove the parsley and bay leaves.

3. Preheat the broiler. Pour the hot soup into a large earthenware casserole. Lay the bread over the soup, cover with the Gruyère and then the Parmigiano-Reggiano, then broil until the cheese is melted and bubbling. Serve immediately!

Winter Vegetable Chowder

MAKES ABOUT
3 QUARTS

This handsome one-bowl meal features winter roots and tubers in a milky broth that's been steeped with aromatics. Turnips, parsnips, rutabagas, leeks, potatoes, a few celery stalks, carrots, and celery root are all candidates for inclusion. You needn't use all at once, but try to include some of the golden-fleshed rutabagas and light green celery and be sure to cut everything in large, handsome shapes.

Bread, toasted and covered with Gruyère or Cantal cheese, sits beneath the vegetables and their broth, building up the soup's heartiness and flavor.

You'll want about 4½ pounds vegetables (unpeeled) plus ½ pound carrots for this much soup. It makes supper for six, but if you're serving less of it, you can, as you work your way through the pot, puree the vegetables at some point to turn the rest into a smooth soup.

THE MILK AND AROMATICS

2 cups milk

4 large parsley branches

1 large thyme sprig or 2 pinches of dried

2 bay leaves

½ onion, sliced

1 garlic clove, halved

10 peppercorns, lightly crushed with 5 juniper berries

THE SOUP

3 tablespoons butter

4 leeks, about an inch across, white parts plus 1 inch of the greens, sliced
    diagonally about 1 inch thick and rinsed

8 to 10 cups vegetables (see headnote), peeled and cut into bold, attractive pieces

2 cups or 10 ounces carrots, peeled and left whole if only 3 inches long, otherwise
    cut into large pieces

2 bay leaves

2 tablespoons chopped parsley

Sea salt and freshly ground pepper

3 tablespoons flour

6 large slices country bread, toasted

Grated or sliced Gruyère or Cantal cheese to cover the toast

Chopped parsley or tarragon or a mixture to finish

1. Put all the ingredients for the milk and aromatics in a saucepan, slowly bring to a boil, then turn off the heat. Cover and set aside while you prepare the vegetables.

2. Melt the butter in a wide soup pot. Add the vegetables, bay leaves, and parsley and sprinkle with 1½ teaspoons salt. Cook over medium heat for 5 minutes or so to heat them up, gently moving them about the pan.

3. Stir in the flour, then add 5 cups water. Bring to a boil, then lower the heat and simmer, partially covered, until the vegetables are tender but still a tad firm, 15 to

A medium-bodied California Merlot would be an appropriate choice. We are partial to Napa Valley's Two Tone Farm.

20 minutes. Strain the milk into a blender, add 1 cup of the vegetables, and puree until smooth. Add the puree back to the soup. Taste for salt and season with pepper.

4. To serve, lay a piece of toast in each bowl, cover it with grated cheese, spoon the soup with its liquid on top, and sprinkle with the chopped herbs.

Cream of Tomato Soup
with souffléed cheese toasts

This quick soup, an American classic, makes a fine pairing with a grilled cheese sandwich or crisp romaine salad. Here the grilled cheese sandwich takes a different form—a souffléed Cheddar topping on a good piece of toasted sandwich bread.

Use an organic brand of tomatoes, one that's thick with puree as well as chunks of tomato.

2$\frac{1}{2}$ tablespoons butter
1 small onion, chopped
1 celery rib, chopped
1$\frac{1}{2}$ teaspoons dried basil, crumbled between your fingers
Pinch of ground cloves
2 tablespoons flour
Two 15-ounce cans diced tomatoes in puree or juice
Pinch of baking soda
2$\frac{1}{2}$ cups Vegetable Stock (page 13) or water
1$\frac{1}{2}$ cups milk
Sea salt and freshly ground pepper
Tomato paste if needed

1 egg, separated, or 1 egg white only

1 teaspoon Dijon mustard

Pinch of cayenne

1 cup grated sharp Cheddar cheese

1 teaspoon minced scallion or shallot

4 slices sandwich bread, lightly toasted

1. Melt the butter in a soup pot over medium heat. Add the onion, celery, basil, and cloves; cook, stirring occasionally, until the onion is limp, about 5 minutes. Stir in the flour, then add the tomatoes, baking soda, and stock. Bring to a boil, lower the heat, and simmer, partially covered, for 20 minutes. Let cool briefly, then puree in a blender until smooth.

2. Preheat the oven to 400°F. Return the soup to the pot, add the milk, and season with salt. If the soup is too thick, thin it with additional milk or stock. If the tomato flavor isn't as rich as you'd like (if the tomatoes were packed in water instead of puree), deepen it by stirring in a little tomato paste.

3. For the toasts, combine the yolk, if you're using it, with the mustard and cayenne, then stir in the cheese. Whisk the white until it holds soft peaks and fold it into the mixture along with the scallion. Spread the mixture on the toasted bread and bake until puffed and golden, about 5 minutes, while you reheat the soup. Serve the soup piping hot, with a piece of cheese toast, cut in half on the diagonal, and fresh pepper ground into each bowl.

Pinot Meunier, a red grape usually used in sparkling wines, is also available as a still wine, such as that made by California's Domaine Chandon. Give it a try with this classic soup.

winter vegetable soups

Passato of Vegetables
with chard and croutons

When Giuliano Bugialli came out with *The Fine Art of Italian Cooking,* his *Passato di Verdura* was one I referenced often at Greens, gradually straying from his ingredients but retaining the method, which is to cook the vegetables slowly in their own juices, adding liquid only as needed to transform them into soup. Early winter is the time to turn to this delicious soup, while cabbage and chard from the farmers' market have that extra measure of flavor that comes with truly fresh food. This mixture results in a dark green soup with a shimmer of red-orange from the carrot and tomato.

If you don't want a soup that's puree smooth—I like a little texture myself— be sure to peel the celery so that the finished soup is free of any stray fibers that might otherwise mar its loveliness.

¼ cup extra virgin olive oil
1 small red or yellow onion, finely diced
1 carrot, sliced
2 celery ribs, peeled if stringy, chopped
1 small potato, peeled and diced
1 large ripe tomato, peeled, seeded, and chopped, or ½ cup diced canned tomato
8 chard leaves, stems removed, the rest roughly chopped (about 8 cups)
1 garlic clove, sliced
Sea salt and freshly ground pepper
Fresh lemon juice to taste

TO FINISH

1 cup small bread cubes
Extra virgin olive oil
Parmigiano-Reggiano, for shaving

An Italian light red, such as a Montepulciano, would be our choice for this soup.

1. Warm the oil in a pot with a tight-fitting lid. Add the vegetables, season with ¾ teaspoon salt, then cover the pot and cook over low heat for 30 minutes, during which the vegetables will produce quite a bit of delicious juice. While they are cooking, bring 1 quart water to a boil.

2. Carefully puree the cooked vegetables with the hot water, beginning with a small amount and adding more, up to 3 or 4 cups, depending on the thickness you want. Leave a little texture or make the soup smooth, as you wish. Return it to the heat, taste for salt, and season with pepper. Add lemon juice to sharpen the flavors.

3. Crisp the bread cubes in a little olive oil over medium-low heat (or in the oven) until golden, 8 to 10 minutes. Ladle the soup into bowls, drizzle with a little olive oil, and add the croutons. Shave the cheese over the top and serve.

Potato and Green Chile Stew
with cilantro cream

MAKES ABOUT
2 QUARTS

This chunky stew is good at any time of the year, but it's winter when you're likely to especially embrace its warming qualities.

This dish is served with a dollop of sour cream that's been mixed with fresh cilantro, blanched first to keep its color. You can also add little cheese dumplings—see the variation. Chicken stock is more traditional than water for the liquid. Use whichever you prefer.

6 long New Mexican, Anaheim, or poblano chiles

2 teaspoons coriander seeds

2 tablespoons sunflower seed or other vegetable oil

1 large onion, diced

2 pounds potatoes, a mixture of russet and other varieties, or all russet, peeled and
    cut into 1½-inch chunks

1 large garlic clove, chopped

Sea salt and freshly ground pepper

6 cups water or chicken stock

Small handful of cilantro

½ cup sour cream

1. Roast the chiles directly over a flame or under the broiler until the skins are bubbly and partially charred. Put them in a bowl, cover them with a plate, and set aside to steam while you peel and chunk the potatoes. Toast the coriander in a dry skillet over medium heat until fragrant and the color starts to dull, about 2 minutes, then cool on a plate and grind to a powder in a spice mill.

2. Heat the oil in a wide soup pot and add the onion, potatoes, and coriander. Turn to coat with the oil, then cook over medium heat, stirring occasionally, until golden in places, about 8 minutes. Meanwhile, slip the skins off the chiles, scrape out the seeds, and chop the flesh into large pieces. Add to the potatoes along with the garlic, 1 teaspoon salt, and the liquid. Give everything a stir, bring to a boil, then lower the heat and simmer. Cover the pot and cook until the potatoes are completely softened, about 25 minutes. Taste for salt and season with pepper. If you want to thicken the broth, mash some of the potatoes right in the pot.

3. Bring a small amount of water to a boil, submerge the cilantro for a few seconds, then drain, rinse under cold water, and pat dry. Chop it finely, then stir it into the sour cream. Serve the stew with a dollop of sour cream in each bowl.

For potatoes, I like to use a mixture. Russets are good because they fall apart and thicken the mixture, but it's also nice to have some big chunks of waxy-fleshed boiling potatoes. You can even slip in some of the new pink-fleshed varieties.

With Cheese Dumplings

Once when making this dish I had some leftover fried queso fresco. Cold, it was rubbery and unappealing; still, I didn't want to throw it out. I added it to the stew, and it melted into tender dumplings. To make these from scratch, simply brown a ½-inch slab of queso blanco or halloumi cheese on both sides in a cast-iron or nonstick pan. Cool, cut into small cubes, then add them to the soup.

Fundamental Squash Soup
with sage

This is a very clean,
simple soup,
embellished only with
a fried sage leaf and
some crisp croutons.
Here, it is vegan.
However, squash is
always good with
browned butter and
various cheeses, such
as Fontina, Gruyère, a
very delicate goat
cheese, and blues.

Steaming winter squash for a soup keeps the purity of its flavor and the brilliance of its color intact. It also spares you the struggle of peeling and chopping what can be a difficult vegetable. You simply halve the creature, put the seeds, a slice of onion, and a sprig of thyme in the water, which will become stock, then steam the squash over the water until tender. The cooked flesh needs just another twenty minutes or so to become a soup. If you make a lot of squash soups using this method, you will see how much varieties differ from one another in sweetness, moisture, texture, color, and flavor.

THE SOUP

1 winter squash or cooking pumpkin (about 3 pounds), halved

2 onions, $\frac{1}{2}$ onion sliced and the remainder finely diced

2 thyme sprigs or $\frac{1}{2}$ teaspoon dried

3 tablespoons olive oil, toasted sunflower seed oil, or butter, browned until it
    smells nutty

2 tablespoons chopped parsley

1 tablespoon chopped sage leaves or 1 teaspoon dried

Sea salt and freshly ground pepper

TO FINISH

$1\frac{1}{2}$ tablespoons *each* olive oil and butter or all oil

8 sage leaves

1 cup small bread cubes

*For wine, go for a not-
too-cumbersome white,
such as a California
Pinot Blanc.*

1. Scoop out the squash seeds. Put them in a wide pot with the sliced onion, 1 thyme sprig or $\frac{1}{4}$ teaspoon dried thyme, and as much water—up to 2 quarts—as you can before putting in a steaming basket. Place the squash on the basket cut side down, bring the water to a boil, then cover and steam until the flesh is tender, anywhere from 30 to 60 minutes, depending on the variety of squash and its size. Reserve the steaming water. When it's done, scoop out the flesh. A 3-pound squash will yield about 4 cups cooked flesh. Strain the steaming water and set it aside.

2. While the squash is steaming, heat the oil in a wide soup pot and add the finely diced onion with the remaining thyme sprig or $\frac{1}{4}$ teaspoon dried thyme, the parsley, and the sage. Cook over medium-low heat, stirring occasionally, until the onions are golden, about 20 minutes. Add the cooked squash, $1\frac{1}{2}$ teaspoons salt, and enough of the reserved liquid to achieve the texture you like. A very dry-fleshed vegetable, such as the Hokkaido pumpkin, will need more liquid than a sugar pumpkin or Red Kuri squash. Mash the squash into the liquid and simmer, covered, for 20 minutes. Pass the soup through a food mill or puree it, then return it to the pot. Taste for salt and season with pepper.

3. To finish, heat the oil and butter in a small skillet. When hot, add the sage leaves and fry until dark green, about 30 seconds. Transfer them to a plate. Add the bread cubes to the pan and cook over medium heat, tossing occasionally, until crisp and golden, about 5 minutes.

4. Ladle the soup into bowls. Add a cluster of croutons to each, 1 or 2 sage leaves, and a bit of freshly ground pepper and serve.

Other Embellishments for Fundamental Squash Soup

- Add 3 small spoonfuls of mascarpone, Robiola, or very mild goat cheese to each bowl.
- Stir in cubes of Fontina or cave-aged Gruyère before serving.
- Finish with finely minced flat-leaf parsley instead of sage. It has a sharp, clean taste that is welcome with squash.
- Garnish with a few drops of roasted pumpkin seed oil.

Squash Soup
with blue cheese and walnut toasts

Served with—or floating in—Fundamental Squash Soup, the luscious blue cheese and walnut toasts bring the sweet, nutty, and salty flavors together in one bite. This pairing is one of my longtime favorites.

Fundamental Squash Soup (page 198)
8 slices baguette or country bread, thinly sliced
$\frac{1}{4}$ pound Point Reyes blue, Maytag blue, or Gorgonzola cheese
3 tablespoons butter at room temperature
$\frac{1}{4}$ cup finely chopped walnuts
Freshly ground pepper

1. Make the squash soup, omitting the croutons.

2. Toast the bread under the broiler until nicely browned on one side, then turn and brown a little less on the second side. Mash the cheese and butter together, then add three-quarters of the walnuts. Spread on the paler side of the toast, then broil until the cheese is bubbling. Remove, dust with the remaining nuts, add a little pepper, and serve with the soup.

The blue cheese and walnuts on the toast here call for a slightly sweeter white, such as an Oregon Pinot Gris.

Cheese and Broccoli Soup

MAKES 6 CUPS

My neighbor, whose family has run a restaurant in Santa Fe for more than sixty years, calls cheese soup a "man's soup"—one of those hearty, rich, stick-to-your-ribs, overly caloric foods. But I think you'll agree that this one, while robust enough for a man's appetite, is light enough for a woman's too. It's right in the middle—not too rich or cheesy, yet distinctly yummy, and the fact that it's based on broccoli makes it extra-nourishing.

1¼ pounds broccoli, about 4 "trees"

Sea salt and freshly ground pepper

3 tablespoons butter or canola oil

1 onion, chopped

1 celery rib, celery diced and leaves chopped

½ pound yellow-fleshed potatoes such as Yukon Gold or Yellow Finn, peeled
    unless organic and diced

1 plump garlic clove, chopped

⅛ teaspoon cayenne, or more to taste

Aromatics: 1 teaspoon dried marjoram, 1 bay leaf, 1 pinch of dried thyme

1 tablespoon flour

½ cup light cream, milk, or reserved cooking water from the broccoli

2 teaspoons Dijon-style mustard, or to taste

2 cups grated sharp Cheddar cheese

Rye or whole wheat bread, toasted

Cheddar is always good with beer and ale.

1. Separate the crowns from the broccoli stems, then separate the crowns into florets. You should have at least 4 cups or a little extra. Thickly peel the stems, quarter them, and chop into small pieces, yielding a cup or so. Bring a quart of water to a boil and add 1 scant teaspoon salt and the broccoli florets. Cook for about 3 minutes, then scoop out the florets, reserving the water. Rinse under cool water and set aside.

2. Melt the butter in a soup pot and add the onion, celery, potato, broccoli stems, garlic, cayenne, and aromatics. Cook over medium-high heat for about 5 minutes, stirring now and then. Add ½ teaspoon salt, stir in the flour, then pour in 3 cups of the reserved water from the broccoli, saving any remainder. Bring to a boil, lower the heat, and simmer, covered, until the potato is tender, 10 to 12 minutes. Add the cream or additional broccoli water if needed to thin the soup. During the last few minutes, add the florets and allow them to heat through.

3. Remove the bay leaf, puree the soup, and return it to the pot. Stir in the mustard, then taste for salt and season with pepper. Just before serving, stir in the cheese, but don't let the soup boil or the cheese will toughen. Serve with the toast on the side or broken into the soup.

Three Variations

- Make this using cauliflower or the lime-green broccoli Romanesco—the flavor will be about the same, but the color will be more lively.
- Try another kind of cheese. A goat's milk Cheddar could be very interesting here. Gruyère and aged sharp Gouda are other possibilities.
- Use a teaspoon of curry powder as a seasoning—it's kind of old-fashioned, but nice and always good.

Green Cabbage Soup
with potatoes and sour cream

MAKES 7 TO 8 CUPS

This shimmering green soup consists only of one small cabbage, a leek, a potato, and, if you like, a dollop of sour cream or yogurt. Light and delicious—especially for so few ingredients—and lovely to look at, it's a soup you can count on having ready to eat in less than thirty minutes, and it's subject to a few excellent variations.

I have tried some traditional recipes that fall along similar lines, in which the cabbage is cooked for hours and then mashed into a puree, and have concluded that this fresher, brighter version is more to our taste today.

THE SOUP

1 small green cabbage, preferably Savoy (about 1 pound)
2 to 3 tablespoons butter
1 large leek, white part only, quartered lengthwise, chopped, and rinsed
1 hefty Yukon Gold or russet potato, peeled and roughly cubed
Sea salt and freshly ground pepper

Sour cream or yogurt
Minced parsley or dill

Serve this soup with an aromatic white from northern Italy, such as a Pinot Grigio from the Alto Adige or a Tocai from Friuli.

1. Quarter the cabbage, remove the cores, and thinly slice the wedges crosswise. You should have 5 to 6 cups. Bring 3 quarts water to a boil, add the cabbage, cook for 1 minute, then drain.

2. Melt the butter in a soup pot. Add the leek and potato, give them a stir, and cook for a minute or two, then add the cabbage and 1 teaspoon salt. Pour over 5 cups water, bring to a boil, then lower the heat and simmer, covered, for 20 minutes or until the potato is tender. Taste for salt and season with pepper.

3. Ladle the soup into bowls, then add to each a dollop of sour cream, a sprinkling of parsley, and a final grinding of pepper.

Four Variations

- Add 5 juniper berries and 2 teaspoons finely chopped rosemary to the leek and potato. Serve the soup with an extra pinch of rosemary.
- Reduce the water by ½ cup and at the end replace the sour cream with crème fraîche or cream.
- Serve with toasted whole wheat bread covered with thinly shaved Cantal cheese or with the Blue Cheese and Walnut Toasts on page 201, using Roquefort, Gorgonzola, or Point Reyes blue. The toasts can be served on the side or put in a soup plate and the soup poured over them.
- Turn the soup into a panade—see page 101.

Sweet Potato and Quince Bisque

These large, easy-to-handle tubers readily suggest themselves as a prime soup ingredient. Yet their intrinsic sweetness makes them a challenge to work with. I've finally decided that a quince (or a tart apple) is what it takes to subdue those sugars and let the more earthy flavors march forward, since quinces are fruity and fragrant yet uncompromisingly tart. Simmer the peels and core for fifteen minutes or so to extract even more of their essence.

I've never found an appropriate garnish for this soup. It doesn't really cry out for anything—not lime, ginger, cilantro, or chile, although none would do any harm. Gruyère and goat cheese, so good with sweet winter squash, aren't really needed here either, so in the end I serve it with nothing.

1 large quince
1 bay leaf
Few pinches of dried thyme
2 pounds (2 or 3) sweet potatoes, such as Jewel, Garnet, or Diana, more or less,
    preferably organic
1 celery rib, diced
1 tablespoon butter plus 1 tablespoon sunflower seed or roasted sesame oil
1 large onion, chopped
Sea salt and freshly ground pepper
1 cup dry white wine
1 cup light cream or half-and-half, optional

1. Peel the quince, then cut it into chunks, working around the core. Put the peels and cores in a pan with 5 cups water, a bay leaf, and a pinch of thyme. Bring to a boil while you peel the sweet potatoes, then add the peels to the pot along with a few sprigs of leaves from the celery rib or a small piece of celery. When the water boils, lower the heat and simmer for about 25 minutes. Meanwhile, chop the sweet potatoes into ½-inch chunks and set aside.

2. Melt the butter with the oil in a wide soup pot over medium-high heat. When hot, add the onion, chunks of quince, sweet potatoes, celery, another pinch of

For sweet potatoes, choose those with red, moist flesh rather than Japanese types, such as Kotobuki. While the latter are certainly delicious with their not-so-sweet chestnut flavor, they can be gummy in a soup.

Fuller-bodied, rounded Sauvignon Blancs blended with Sémillon, such as those made by Duckhorn and Spottswoode in Napa Valley, have sweet and tart elements that pair well with the same notes in this soup.

thyme, and 1 teaspoon salt. Give everything a stir and cook, partially covered, stirring occasionally, for 15 to 20 minutes, or until a glaze has built up on the surface of the pan and the vegetables have begun to color in places. Pour in the wine and scrape the bottom of the pan to deglaze the sugars, creating a caramel-colored liquid. After a few minutes, when the wine has reduced by half or so, pour the stock through a strainer right over the vegetables. Reduce the heat so that it's cooking at a slow boil, cover the pan, and cook until the quince and sweet potatoes have softened, about 25 minutes.

3. Puree the soup until smooth and return it to the pan. Season with another teaspoon of salt, or to taste, and pepper. Stir in the cream if you're using it, then serve.

MAKES ABOUT
1 QUART

Celery and Celery Root Soup
with shiitake mushrooms

The trimmings of the soup vegetables make an excellent little stock in a very short time. Start it first.

Mushrooms (and truffles) resonate particularly well with celeriac. Both possess a dank, earthy flavor. You can make this soup into bisque (see the variation), but I prefer it more textured, with bits of vegetables, the beautiful mushrooms, and pale green celery leaves. If you plan to make a pureed soup, you can cut everything more roughly.

THE STOCK

Celery root peels (see Note on page 208)
Leek roots plus 1 cup pale greens
Small handful of parsley stems
Several ends of celery ribs plus darker celery leaves
Stems from the shiitake mushrooms
Any other vegetables from the basic Vegetable Stock recipe (page 13), including a
    few dried shiitake mushrooms

1 celery root, trimmed of its leaves (about 1 pound)
1 long leek, trimmed of root and greens (about 3½ ounces)
3 tablespoons butter
1 celery rib, peeled if stringy and attractively sliced
Sea salt and freshly ground pepper
1 lemon, halved
½ cup cream or half-and-half, optional
4 shiitake mushrooms, caps thinly sliced
Small handful of pale green celery leaves, slivered

1. Put the stock ingredients in a pot and cover with 6 cups water. Bring to a boil, then lower the heat and simmer, partially covered, while you prepare the soup vegetables and start the soup. Cut the peeled celery root into an uneven ½-inch dice. Slice the leek lengthwise into quarters, then chop and rinse well.

2. Melt 2 tablespoons of the butter in a wide soup pot over medium heat, letting it brown a little, then add the celery root, leek, and celery. Season with ½ teaspoon salt, give everything a stir, cover the pan, and reduce the heat a little. Cook for about 10 minutes, checking once or twice to make sure nothing is sticking or browning. If so, add a little water or splash of white wine.

3. Pour the soup stock through a strainer into a 1-quart measuring cup, then pour it into the vegetables. Bring to a boil, lower the heat, and simmer, covered, for 20 minutes, or until the vegetables are soft but not mushy. Taste for salt—it will need more—and squeeze in the juice of half the lemon. Add the cream, if using.

4. Melt the remaining tablespoon of butter in a medium skillet and add the mushrooms. Season with a pinch or two of salt, squeeze a few drops of lemon juice over them, and sauté over medium-high heat until browned and tender.

5. Ladle the soup into soup plates, divide the mushrooms among them, and garnish with the celery leaves and pepper.

Try a low-alcohol, elegant French Chardonnay or a Chardonnay-Sémillon blend from Washington State, such as L'Ecole No. 41 or Columbia Crest.

winter vegetable soups

Puree the soup vegetables, add the cream, and season with salt and lemon to taste. Serve garnished with the mushrooms, celery leaves, and pepper.

Note: To peel a celery root, first wash it well to rinse away the dirt, then, using a sharp knife, simply saw away the skin as if you were peeling an orange. Be sure to cut deeply where the roots are amassed, because this is also where sand collects. However, these gnarly parts are full of flavor and should go right into the stock.

MAKES ABOUT
2 QUARTS

Celery Root and Apple Soup
with lovage and blue cheese

A crisp apple adds welcome tartness and acidity to the earthy celery root, while the tiny salad garnish of slivered celery, lovage, and blue cheese is fresh and crunchy.

Start a vegetable stock so that you can use the flavorful celery root skins. Both leeks and onions are good in this soup; you can use them in tandem or interchangeably.

THE STOCK

Scrubbed peels from the celery root
1 cup chopped leek greens or onion
3 long celery ribs, chopped
1 carrot, chopped
Bouquet garni: 1 bay leaf, 3 parsley sprigs, pinch of dried thyme
Sea salt

THE SOUP

2 tablespoons butter
1 onion or 2 fat leeks, thinly sliced
3 cups diced celery root (1 to 1½ pounds scrubbed celery root)
1 cup diced celery ribs
1 large tart apple, such as Granny Smith, peeled and thinly sliced

$^{1}/_{2}$ cup diced potato
1 cup half-and-half or milk

$^{3}/_{4}$ cup very thinly sliced celery heart
$^{1}/_{4}$ apple, thinly sliced then slivered
5 small lovage leaves, slivered
1 ounce or so blue cheese, crumbled

1. Thickly slice away the celery root skins with a sharp knife. Cut especially deeply at the base, where there's likely to be fine dirt swirled into the folds of the roots. Put these trimmings in a pot with the rest of the stock ingredients, including $^{1}/_{2}$ teaspoon salt and 6 cups water. Bring to a boil, then lower the heat and simmer, covered, while you get the soup started, giving it 25 minutes if time allows.

    The saltiness of the blue cheese garnish would be balanced nicely by the acidity and fruit of a German Riesling.

2. Melt the butter in a wide soup pot. Add the onion, celery root, celery, apple, and potato. Sprinkle with 1 teaspoon salt, give everything a stir, and cook over medium heat, turning the contents of the pan occasionally, for about 10 minutes. Add $^{1}/_{2}$ cup water, cover the pan, and cook over low heat until the stock has finished cooking, or for about 10 minutes. The apple and onion will have caramelized a little.

3. Pour the stock through a strainer right into the vegetables. Cover and simmer until the vegetables are completely soft, about 20 minutes. Puree until smooth, then return the soup to the pot. Stir in the half-and-half and taste for salt.

4. Serve the soup in shallow bowls. Toss the finishing ingredients together and place a small mound in each bowl.

✓Rutabaga and Leek Chowder
with crisp smoky croutons

Here's a pale golden, utterly creamy but creamless soup that will confound your friends. "Rutabagas?" they'll ask when you tell them what it's made of. Those poor old things? Frankly, I've always been a fan. They taste a lot like turnips, which is to say sweet and rooty; they're a pretty color beneath their skins, and, like turnips, they take well to smoky flavors, such as bacon and ham. The smoky element in this recipe comes from Spanish smoked paprika (page 92), which is lodged into crisped buttery croutons. If you prefer to skip the croutons, you can, instead, melt a tablespoon or two of butter, stir in $1/4$ to $1/2$ teaspoon smoked paprika, then drizzle it into the soup.

THE SOUP $1^1/2$ pounds rutabagas — *celeriac*   *' cutting celery*
2 to 3 tablespoons butter
Hefty pinch of dried thyme
1 bay leaf
2 medium leeks, chopped (1 to 2 cups) *+ cutting celery stalks*
One $1/4$-pound potato, peeled and cut into 1-inch cubes
Sea salt and freshly ground pepper
6 cups Vegetable Stock (page 13) or water

TO FINISH 2 tablespoons butter
1 cup 1-inch bread chunks
$1/2$ teaspoon Spanish smoked paprika

A full-bodied, aromatic white, such as an Alsatian Riesling or an Austrian Grüner Veltliner, can stand up to the smoke and creamy elements here.

1. Thickly peel the rutabagas, getting under the epidermis, quarter them lengthwise, then slice crosswise about $3/8$ inch thick.

2. Melt the butter in a wide soup pot with the thyme and bay leaf. Let it brown a little, then add the leeks. Give a stir and cook over medium heat for 3 or 4 minutes, then add the rutabagas and potato. Toss in a teaspoon of salt and cook, partially covered, until everything has wilted down, 5 minutes or so. Add the stock,

bring to a boil, lower the heat, and simmer, covered, until the rutabagas are tender but not mushy—you'll want some texture—20 to 25 minutes.

3. Puree half the vegetables and return them to the pot. Or puree the whole batch for a completely smooth soup. Taste for salt and season with pepper.

4. Melt the remaining butter in a small skillet over medium-high heat. Add the bread chunks, toss them in the butter, then reduce the heat and cook until crisp and golden, after 5 to 8 minutes. Add the smoked paprika, toss the croutons, then turn off the heat. Serve the soup with croutons in each bowl and a delicate sprinkling of extra paprika over the top.

Spinach-Sorrel Soup
with mushroom toasts

Mushrooms have a cozy affinity for both spinach and sorrel, which I know from having paired them together over the years in sauces, timbales, salads, and side dishes. Here I cook the greens in the Mushroom Stock and serve the soup with mushroom duxelles on toast, which you can either eat out of hand or drop into the soup, where they become big, mushroomy croutons. If you don't have sorrel, make the soup without it and add a few drops of lemon juice or white wine vinegar to sharpen the flavors.

THE SOUP

2 tablespoons butter plus 2 teaspoons olive oil
1 large onion, thinly sliced
1 garlic clove, sliced
Leaves from 3 marjoram branches or $\frac{1}{2}$ teaspoon dried
2 bunches of spinach, stems discarded and leaves washed (about 12 cups packed)
4 cups sorrel leaves (about 3 ounces), optional
Sea salt and freshly ground pepper

5 cups Mushroom Stock (page 14)

1 slice firm country bread, torn into large pieces

Fresh lemon juice or vinegar to taste

$\frac{1}{4}$ cup cream

$\frac{1}{2}$ pound mushrooms

2 tablespoons butter

1 large shallot, finely diced

1 small garlic clove, minced

2 tablespoons sherry

3 to 4 slices firm country bread

I like to drizzle a teaspoon or so of cream into each serving, where it blossoms over the surface. If cream isn't in your diet plan, you might stir a spoonful of yogurt into each serving instead or simply serve it with only the mushroom toasts.

1. Melt the butter with the oil in a wide soup pot until foaming and just starting to brown around the edges. Add the onion, garlic, and marjoram and stir frequently as you cook over medium-high heat, wilting the onion and browning it just a little so that you get that good "fried" onion smell, about 5 minutes. Add the spinach and sorrel if you're using it and sprinkle with a teaspoon of salt. When it's wilted down, after about 3 minutes, add the stock and the bread. Bring to a boil, lower the heat, and simmer gently for 15 minutes.

2. Puree the soup until smooth and return it to the pan. Taste for salt; add lemon juice to taste (even if you did use sorrel). Stir in half of the cream.

For wine, open a bottle of spicy, peppery California Syrah from Pasa Robles, such as Alban or the more affordable Justin.

3. Make the mushroom toasts. Put the mushrooms in a food processor and pulse until finely chopped. Heat the butter in a medium skillet, add the shallot and garlic, and cook over medium heat for a minute, then add the mushrooms and raise the heat. Season with a few pinches of salt and some pepper, then cook, stirring frequently, as the mushrooms release their juices and then start to dry out. Add the sherry and cook for several minutes more. Taste for salt. Toast the bread, spread the mushrooms over the top, and cut into small pieces. If there are extra mushrooms, add them to the soup.

4. Serve the soup and drizzle the remaining cream into each bowl. Grind some pepper over the top and serve. Pass the mushroom toasts.

Doctoring Up Canned Soups

While there's nothing better than a homemade soup, a good canned soup can take its place when you have no time to cook. Even while working on this book, I found myself occasionally opening a can of soup for my lunch while squash was roasting or beans were soaking for a soup to be made later in the day.

I'm thrilled that there are good prepared soups today and that many are made of organic ingredients. They've come a long way from those oversalted broths enhanced with dehydrated vegetables, but they can still use some doctoring. Here are a few tricks I use to turn a soup in a can into something that's just a little bit more interesting.

FOR LENTIL SOUPS OR MINESTRONES

A few drops of good, fragrant olive oil and a grind of black pepper
Thin slices of Parmesan cheese
Toast rubbed with garlic and torn into small pieces
A bit of minced parsley or other herb or a spoonful of Salsa Verde (page 142)
Leftover noodles
A few slivered spinach leaves

FOR BLACK BEAN SOUPS

Chopped cilantro or Cilantro Salsa (page 153)
Coconut milk
Finely chopped green chile
Chipotle chile, either powdered or in adobo sauce, or minced serrano
Cream or half-and-half, lemon, and parsley

A tiny pinch of cloves with the lemon and parsley
Sherry
Hard-cooked egg, chopped

Cream or milk, including soy milk
Buttered toast, cut into squares, toasted bread crumbs, or croutons
Minced herbs, such as tarragon, basil, chives, and dill
Curry powder
Sharp Cheddar cheese melted over whole wheat toast
Croutons spread with goat cheese, sprinkled with thyme, and broiled
Pesto (page 154)

Fresh lime or lemon juice
Few drops of aged red wine, Chardonnay, or sherry vinegar
Minced scallions, chile, and cilantro
Diced avocado
Diced roasted red peppers
Yogurt or sour cream
Basil puree or pesto (page 154)
Minced dill, opal basil, marjoram, or lovage
Cilantro Salsa (page 153)

Few drops of olive oil or roasted sesame oil
Minced rosemary or tarragon
Lemon zest and lemon juice
Croutons or toasted bread crumbs
Few drops of soy sauce
Salsa Verde (page 142)

A Passion for Pottery

About the same time that I became interested in cooking, at the age of fifteen, I became interested in ceramics. In fact, as I was learning to bake bread I was also learning to throw clay, and the two—baking and ceramics—were often intermingled in my mind as equivalent art forms. Eventually my work became food related, but I've always maintained a passion for pottery. I never think of food separately from the dish it's going to be served on or buy a piece of pottery without seeing it with food on it, for shape, color, and pattern work in harmony with each other and food to show it at its best.

I'm drawn to a mixture that includes, among other things, old Haviland, Ginori, and Limoges dishes, whose classic lines are irrefutably exquisite. I also like funky stuff, such as old platters and bowls from Mexico. But mostly my taste gravitates to the decorative qualities and the relaxed charm found in folk art ceramics. I've been very fortunate to have as a good friend the ultimate passionate pottery person, Judith Espinar, whose Santa Fe store The Clay Angel has provided thousands of customers with beautiful works in clay, many from small, artisanal studios in France, Italy, Hungary, and Mexico. These are dishes that share some of the same characteristics of the foods I like—they're nonindustrial products that expose the flavor of tradition and the hand and eye of an individual potter or studio. They are the equivalent of those artisanal, handmade foods that are linked to a particular producer, a method, a story, or a place. Both dishes and foods like these stand apart from their mass-produced equivalent, and Judith puts as much passion into making sure these traditional crafts thrive as I do for foods that share these characteristics.

In addition to traditional potters, there are modern ceramists, artists who make one-of-a-kind works rather than run production studios. I had pretty much forgotten about contemporary ceramics until I met Vicki Snyder, my neighbor. The first time I went to her house I was dazzled by her vast collection of contemporary clay works, including her own slip-and-soda pieces. I immediately saw how exciting it would be to use some of these pieces in this book and to mix them with work from Judith's collection and some traditional tableware. Vicki, who was also excited by this prospect, ended up being a collaborator of sorts, generously lending me pieces from her collection. One artist, Gail Kendall, even made a highly ornate soup tureen especially for the book. It is a wild, wonderful thing (see page 216) that demands that one aspire to make an equally imaginative soup. All of these dishes are lovely to handle, beautiful to look at, and highly complementary with food.

In addition to recognizing both Judith and Vicki for their devoted passion to ceramics and their keen vision of what's of value and worth saving and making, I want to thank all of the artists whose work appears here. Their names and the addresses of their studios are listed below if you wish to contact them. Other works come from my personal collection or from The Clay Angel in Santa Fe, New Mexico. I hope that seeing such a range of dishes inspires you to see what possibilities exist in your world and to use them to heighten the pleasure of cooking and eating.

Peter Beasecker   page 162
8706 Redondo Dr.
Dallas, TX 75218

Doug Casebeer   page 107
Anderson Ranch Art Center
PO Box 5598
Snowmass, CO 81615

Sam Clarkson   page 54
15 Patrick Rd.
Bonny Doon, CA 95060

Giselle Hicks   page 41
31211 Boca Raton Place
Laguna Niguel, CA 92677

Sarah Jaeger   page 175
908 Broadway
Helena, MT 59601

Gail Kendall   pages 160, 216
3200 Van Dorn St.
Lincoln, NE 68502

Alleghany Meadows   pages 87, 199
73 Rocky Rd.
Carbondale, CO 81623

Brad Miller   page vi (lower right)
606 Westminster Ave.
Venice, CA 90291

Charlotte Morris   page 58
941 Dunlap St.
Santa Fe, NM 87501

Takashi Nakazato   page 46
Anderson Ranch Art Center
PO 5598
Snowmass, CO 81615

Siglinda Scarpa   page 118
The Goathouse Gallery
680 Alton Alston Rd.
Pittsboro, NC 27312
www.siglindascarpa.com

Sandy Simon   page 73
1812 5th St.
Berkeley, CA 94710

Laura Smith   page 92
0060 Little Elk Creek
Snowmass, CO 81654

Vicki Snyder   pages 74, 113, 168
6 Magdalen
Lamy, NM 87540

OTHER SOURCES AND CREDITS

The Clay Angel
125 Lincoln Ave., Suite 111
Santa Fe, NM 84501
505-988-4800
    page 139 Tea cups and plate by
        Jars, France
    page 175 Green and blue dishes by
        Aletha Soulé
    page 118 Bowl by Aletha
        Soulé
    pages 178, 196 Bowls by
        Uriarte, Talavera, Puebla,
        Mexico
    page v Turnip pot by Nathalie
        Hubert

page 182 Pumpkin Tureen by
    Bouthinon, France
page vii Pineapple Tureen by
    Bouthinon, France
page 131 Bowl by Commune aux
    Terre, France

Santa Fe School of Cooking
    pages 48, 155
116 West San Francisco St.
Santa Fe, NM 87501
505-983-4511
www.santafeschoolofcooking.com

World Market   pages 32, 99
Locations nationwide
www.worldmarket.com

MY COLLECTION

    page 173 Contemporary French
        bowl
    page 190 Old French clay ware
    page 152 Old Mexican bowl
        (Puebla) on French Provençal
        plate
    page 89 Green clay bowls from
        Apt, Provence, France
    page 116 Cazuela from
        marketplace, Tlapa, Mexico